Death of the Modern SuperHero

How Grace Breaks our Rules

by Chris Lautsbaugh

PUBLISHED BY PROJECT GRACE PUBLISHING

WWW.NOSUPERHEROES.COM

Chris Lautsbaugh
Project Grace Publishing
2624 NE Winters Rd.
Bremerton WA 98311
www.nosuperheroes.com

Unless otherwise noted, Scripture quotations are taken from The Holy Bible, English Standard Version. Copyright © 2001 by Crossway Bibles, a division of Good News Publishers. All rights reserved.

Cover Design: *Mariana Magno & Brian Diehl*

Cover Art: *Kyle Walters, wwww.kyleart.com*

Interior Design: *De Wet & Marysol Blomerus*, www.blomerus.org

Illustrator: *Sharon Ellis*

Editing: *Joe Bunting, www.joebunting.com*

ISBN: 9780983271000
Library of Congress Control Number: 2011921240

Printed in the United States of America

To recovering superheroes around the world

Acknowledgments

This book has been a work in process for nearly 10 years. My personal journey of grace has been impacted by so many, it would be impossible to mention them all by name. I am certain that I have "stolen" some of their thoughts in these pages without credit being given. For that I apologize. Your thoughts are now woven in with my own to shape my understanding on this topic. There are several that stand out and need to be mentioned for their teachings and writings that have shaped me through the years. Special thanks to Ron & Judy Smith, Mark & Dawn Masucci, Philip Yancey, Jerry Bridges, Brennan Manning, and many, many more.

Thank you to my illustrator Sharon Ellis, cover designers Mariana Magno and Brian Diehl, and typesetters De Wet & Marysol Blomerus. Special thanks to Krista Stauffer, Jennifer Bester, and Jerry Lautsbaugh who painstakingly edited my rough draft.

Thanks is due to Joe Bunting who helped revise the second edition.

The biggest thanks is reserved for my wife and best friend, Lindsey. Thank you for being a beacon of grace in my life every day.

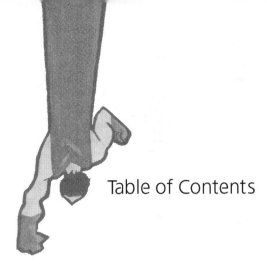

Table of Contents

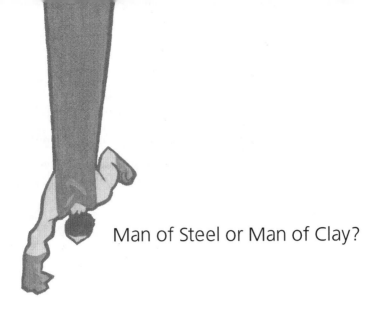

Man of Steel or Man of Clay?

"Superman is dead."

As children we dream of flying through the air like our heroes. In our dreams, we leap tall buildings in a single bound, run at the speed of light, and rush in to save the day from evil villains in the nick of time. Saving the world is all in a day's work.

As rational thinking adults we may cease to dream this way, but how often do we feel like we must be like a superhero in our Christian life? With all the do's and don'ts we see in Scripture and those we hear preached from the pulpit, the obvious conclusion is that we must be more than human.

There's just one problem. Unlike our superhero idols, we are not indestructible.

Over the past 10 years, I have been involved with a Bible school that takes students through all 66 books of the Bible in nine months. At the end of one session we asked the students, "What truth have you come away with that most influenced your life?" After pouring over every chapter and verse in Scripture one student's response was, "Superman is dead." I thought it was a profound statement that summed up the message of Scripture from cover to cover. In fact, it is what makes Christianity different from every other religion and system on the planet.

CLIMBING THE LADDER

From the moment we come out of the womb, modern society begins to condition us to believe success in life involves climbing the ladder. We attempt to succeed in all areas of life, while avoiding things that make us feel weak. As a child, adults prompt us to make the "traveling" or "select" sports team. They encourage us to find ourselves in the gifted classes as early as elementary school. Parents attempt to coax their children to walk faster, talk sooner, and read well beyond the average level. As we strive for this level of success, something is ingrained in our subconscious; a belief system is formed. We begin believing popular mottos such as "nothing is for free" or "hard work brings happiness." Over time we become perfectionists.

As we continue in our journey to adulthood, it becomes nearly impossible to avoid thoughts about climbing the ladder. In business, we speak of the corporate ladder, and we do whatever it takes to make sure we continue on it in an upward direction. In education, this looks like the pursuit of increasingly higher degrees of education. Athletes seek to rise through the ranks of the amateur leagues to the majors. Even upon reaching this pinnacle, the definition of success rises to becoming an All Star; perhaps eventually a legend or a national hero.

⊚ ⊙ ⊚

From the moment we come out of the womb, modern society begins to condition us to believe success in life involves climbing the ladder.

Surprisingly, if we turn our attention to the church, we see a similar picture. Are we content to be in the choir, or must we be the choir director? In Africa, ministers tend to seek as many titles before and after their names as possible. It is not unusual to see a Bishop Apostle Prophet so and so of such and such church. Ministries and missionaries are measured by statistics and newsletter headlines. We often say, "If only one person believes, it is worth it." This may be true, but it will not impress the missions committee in their financial decisions. We must be more than ordinary. We must be superheroes!

I am in no way saying we should strive for something less than the best. I don't believe that this perfectionistic worldview has changed the church's perspective of salvation. No biblical Christian would say we are saved by works. Scripture is clear. Most of us can quote the following verse, "For by grace you have been saved through faith. And this is not your own doing; it is the gift of God, not a result of works, so that no one may boast" (Ephesians 2:8-9).

Salvation is a free gift. There is nothing we can do to deserve it or be worthy of it. This principle distinguishes Christianity from other religions

However, in my years of ministry, I continually meet individuals who subconsciously believe that as soon as they get saved, the rules change. Salvation was free, yet somehow they feel a spiritual version of climbing the ladder becomes necessary to stay in God's good books. Even their spiritual lives become affected. They believe they must become spiritual superheroes.

Superman is Dead

Like many boys, my son, Garett, has a fascination with superheroes. One day my wife, Lindsey, was home with our boys. She dressed our son up in his cape, and let him head off to the land of make believe. He flew around the house for a while before retreating to the back porch. It wasn't long until Lindsey heard a huge crash accompanied by the sounds of a crying boy. Rushing outside, she found a pile of assorted lawn furniture that had been stacked into a platform, designed to be the launching pad for flight. Initially, she was concerned that he had been hurt as he sobbed uncontrollably, but as he calmed down, Lindsey found out the true source of his tears.

He crashed as he attempted to fly. He had the cape, he built the tower, he believed with all his heart he could; still, gravity took effect and he crashed to the ground. Even with his best effort and all his faith, it did not work. The reality of this crushed his three-year-old spirit. He was not a superhero. Garett could not fly.

◉ ◉ ◉

For many of us, the thought of not being a superhero is much worse than the pain of crashing under the weight of our own effort. We try to do the impossible a long time before we will admit our weakness. Depression and burnout are growing to epidemic

For many of us, the thought of not being a superhero is much worse than the pain of crashing under the weight of our own effort.

proportions, especially among people "working for God." In my organization, a verbal survey found 30% of the workers actively taking anti-depressants or sleeping aids. Weakness is something no one wants. We will put on a false face for a long time before admitting our true need. We will work until exhaustion, take medication, or find ways to escape reality before we ever utter the words "I can't do it."

JARS OF CLAY AND SKUBALON

The fact that society exalts displays of strength is not something new to the twenty-first century. Paul dealt with these very things in Second Corinthians.

Corinth was a leading first-century city, steeped in the Greek worldview, a worldview that exalted all the externals, such as knowledge, physical strength, wealth, and eloquence. According to these standards, Paul fell woefully short. Paul, according to many biblical scholars, was a short, balding, annoying sort of fellow, and may have had stomach issues and bad eyesight (these are some of the options for the thorn in the flesh in 2 Cor. 12:7). He was not a skilled speaker and bore on his body the marks of many shipwrecks and beatings.

Yet, Paul knew the true source of his ministry was not his personal talents and abilities. It was to this effect he encouraged the Corinthian believers when he said, "But we have this treasure in jars of clay, to show that the surpassing power belongs to God and not to us" (2 Corinthians 4:7).

Clay jars were as ordinary as grocery sacks are today. They were so common they had no inherent value. The uncommon thing was what filled them. In this illustration, the jars are filled with the Spirit of God. By Paul's definition, a true minister spoke not from his success but from the Spirit inside. This illustration represents what he wanted to occur in the mindset of Corinthian believers. He desired them to know they qualified as ministers, even without all the outward things society told them were necessary.

Paul takes it one step further in Philippians 3:4-9. Philippi was a Greek colony and so the same worldview was prevalent. Look at the radical, counter-culture statements he makes here:

> ...though I myself have reason for confidence in the flesh also. If anyone else thinks he has reason for confidence in the flesh, I have more: circumcised on the eighth day, of the people of Israel, of the tribe of Benjamin, a Hebrew of Hebrews; as to the law, a Pharisee; as to zeal, a persecutor of the church; as to righteousness, under the law blameless. But whatever gain I had, I counted as loss for the sake of Christ. Indeed, I count everything as loss because of the surpassing worth of knowing Christ Jesus my Lord. For his sake I have suffered the loss of all things and count them as rubbish, in order that I may gain Christ and be

found in him, not having a righteousness of my own that comes from the law, but that which comes through faith in Christ, the righteousness from God that depends on faith.

We see Paul listing all the outward attributes and qualifications he could boast of. He speaks of his culture, his passport, his religious training and accomplishments. Look how he explains these things that could be considered "gain." In verse 8, the word he uses to describe these qualifications is "rubbish." The Greek word for this is "skubalon."[1] I don't know many Greek words, but this one sticks in my memory. Skubalon is what is thrown to the dogs. It is dung, filth. Paul says his long list of outward accomplishments is worthy of the sewer. Flush them down the toilet! Our greatest human accomplishments stink when compared to the work of Christ. Righteousness does not come from striving or living a privileged life but through faith. It is a gift of God. We can never add to the work of Christ by our own efforts.

> Skubalon is what is thrown to the dogs... Paul says his long list of outward accomplishments is worthy of the sewer.

Skubalon is where I gather all my best efforts at doing the right thing. I pile these high on a silver platter and lift it heavenward in an act of showing God how committed I am.

"Surely God will look at this great offering and be pleased," I think to myself.

What I often fail to recognize is that what I am holding up to God is merely a silver platter piled high and deep with dung! No serious Christian would ever consider giving God a gift of sewage. Yet, this is what Paul equates our finest efforts at earning God's favor to.

Poop!

It is a disgusting picture, and it smells. Our best attempts to please the Lord emit a foul, foul smell!

After receiving the gift of salvation, we often turn our attention towards living a godly life. The focus quickly turns from the work done on the cross to our responsibility. Yes, God has saved us by grace, but now "we better live right!"

This is communicated subtly and and even sometimes with outright manipulation. Even the best-intentioned believer, with the purest heart, can easily find themselves slipping back to the spiritual version of climbing the ladder.

As believers, we desire to live a life of obedience and holiness. Yet, the reality is that sin does not disappear the moment we receive the precious gift of grace. As we journey in our newfound faith, questions begin to rise in our minds.

"How much is enough?"

"What does it take to make it to heaven?"

"Is it once saved, always saved or does our eternal destiny hang in the balance with every thought and choice?"

"What is required to hear those words "well done, good and faithful servant" on Judgment Day?" (Matthew 25:21).

In my 19 years of ministry I have met many solid believers who ask these questions deep in their hearts. Most are afraid to voice this for fear of the repercussions. These kinds of feelings do not go over well in newsletters or ministry reports.

Moments after a new convert prays the prayer of salvation, we begin telling them the rules. We "disciple" them in how to work hard at being a "good Christian." Often we end up telling them to don the cape and become a superhero.

GRACE OR KARMA?

In his book *Bono on Bono*[2], the lead singer of the Irish rock band U2, shares the most culturally-relevant presentations of the gospel I have heard. He does this without using religious words or catchphrases such as "washed in the blood." Bono explains the world has two main forces—grace and karma. Karma, by definition, is getting what you deserve. If you do good, good things will happen. Similarly if you do wrong, you can expect a negative result. Climbing the ladder is all about karma. If you work hard, you will succeed. The Christianized version of this says if you pray the right prayer or stay away from sin long enough, you can move the hand of God to get what you want. It is a spiritual form of manipulation, but the one being manipulated is God himself! Grace, says Bono, plays by a different set of rules. Grace stands in opposition to karma. We deserve nothing less than hell. Instead God pours out abundant blessings on us. This doesn't make sense. It often seems too good to be true. Surely a grace this big would be abused.

A few years back, I was listening to Philip Yancey, author of the fantastic book *What's So Amazing about Grace?*[3]. He was speaking on the same idea as Bono. Instead of wording it "grace and karma", he chose the terms "grace and gravity." Gravity speaks of weight and rules. Grace is the opposite. As I listened to him describe these concepts, it brought a smile to my face. These ideas were different from everything I had ever known to be true. I inhaled deeply the fresh air of grace as tears came to my eyes. It was so out of the ordinary, so counter culture, so refreshing. Grace takes the rules and turns them upside down.

I have often imagined what I would do if I ran a new believers class at a church. The stereotypical convert is told to "cut his hair, change his music, stop chewing tobacco, drinking alcohol, and stop going out with girls who do these things." These are often good, biblical suggestions taught by sincere saints. However almost overnight, it transforms a relationship with God into a list of do's and don'ts. Immediately we put the new believer on the ladder and prod them with quotes of biblical commands. This turns Christianity into another version of the work-based culture of our world (not to mention every other religious system on the planet). You need to grunt and groan to succeed. Get your hands dirty and make your own salvation.

What if...

What if we really taught new believers the reality of sin, the extent of the gift of the salvation, and the appropriate response of holiness to that gift? What if we taught them that salvation is not a checklist but a relationship? What if we told them it was okay to not be a superhero?

That is the goal of this book.

After we come to terms with the bad news, that we are not superheroes, we will be able to fully explore the good news. God has given us grace, our salvation.

As we begin to understand the problem of sin, salvation will become more clear as well. The world is broken and has been since Genesis 3. Everyone starts in this broken state, everyone is in need of a rescuer. We must first understand sin and the way God deals with it throughout history. I can say with confidence that you will come away with a greater view of God's grace and the gift of salvation as you read these pages.

Our journey wouldn't be complete unless we spoke of what a believer does after salvation. How do we live and grow? We don't want our grace to be "sloppy agape" or "cheap grace." So in this book we will spend a great deal of time looking at holiness and sanctification in response to salvation. We cannot separate these three things; sin, salvation, and sanctification. The biblical writers often dealt with these three issues together and we will do that as well.

Christ is now the Superhero, we are not. Even when we attempt to look good, our best efforts add up to skubalon, worthy only to be flushed into the sewer. The days of us attempting to be a superhero are over. Superman is dead. Grace turns things upside down.

REST IN
PEACE
SUPERHERO

⊙ QUESTIONS
for discussion

In what ways can you identify with "climbing the ladder" or trying to be a superhero? How does that thought pattern creep into our Christian lives?

Which view do you prefer in your life - karma or grace? Do you want to get what you deserve or unmerited favor?

List several ways your relationship with God looks like "karma" or "gravity?" How can you change these?

Encourage yourself with the areas in your life where you find yourself walking in grace.

God Is Not the Bad Guy

I am a coffee lover. Some might even call me a coffee snob. There are very few things in life that I enjoy more than a good cup coffee. I have been in missions for close to 20 years and gone many places where good coffee is as scarce as a flush toilet or a warm shower. Coffee was not meant to be freeze dried or dissolved in hot water. It was meant to be carefully roasted as beans, ground to the perfect grind, steeped for several minutes, and then pressed. That is what makes a good cup of coffee.

Being the experienced traveler that I am, I have found a way to take good coffee with me. I believe in the phrase, "when in Rome, do as the Romans do," except when it comes to the coffee. I am the owner of a travel press and Ziplock bags. Anywhere I can find boiling water I have a good cup of java awaiting me.

The key to the perfect cup of coffee, though, is not the water, or the amount of time you brew the cup, or even the quality of coffee itself. I could take all the perfect ingredients, mix them in the travel press, and get nothing but a cup of sludge. No, the perfect cup requires a filter. I insert the filter to trap the grounds at the bottom. Without the filter, the rest is worthless. No one wants to pick grinds out of their teeth all day long. The filter is the key.

God is like a good cup of coffee. He looks different depending on the what filter you use. We often look at God through the filter of our own culture, our religious background, our experiences, and even our daily emotions. Through this filter, God becomes relative, different for everyone. God is angry or pleased with us depending on what happens during that day. We begin to affirm the cultural norm that says, "Truth is what you make it."

Is He a Schizophrenic?

Is He strict to some and liberal to others?

Does He bless some with a great life and doom others to the pain of rape and abuse?

The only filter that truly reveals God is the Word of God. Any other filter will leave our teeth full of coffee grounds. The Word of God sends delicious, high quality coffee past our lips. Emotions lie. Experiences change. Culture has thousands of interpretations, religion has even more. Truth, however, never changes. God's character never changes.

Many divisions within the church through the centuries have come from different perspectives of God. Some have divided over the idea that God is sovereign and in control. Others fight for a belief that says man has a free will that trumps all. We have Calvinists, Arminians, and Finneyism among others. "Isms" and "ists" develop from these different opinions. Sometimes we change God to get emotionally satisfying answers to the difficulties of life. We often try to explain away the mystery of God. We cannot do that. God does not change. What we need to do is change our questions.

Let's look through the filter of truth, not our own personal lives. Let's allow the Bible to tell us who this God really is. We are going to look at just a few of the traits the Bible shows us about this amazing God. Time and space will limit our exploration, but the truth of God can be found in the pages of Scripture.

Let's look at G. O. D.

G: GOOD, EVEN WHEN IT IS UNEXPECTED

Almost everytime I speak at a conference or a church, if I say the words, "God is good," followed by a pause, I will get the response, "All the time." I come back to the audience "All the time." "God is good" they yell. These words have become so common that we recite them without any thought to the implications. However, let's take a closer look at the flagship verse for this belief, Romans 8:28, which says, "And we know that for those who love God all things work together for good, for those who are called according to his purpose."

You are probably familiar with this verse. It hangs on our refrigerators. It is the part in a greeting card our eyes browse over. Let's do a little digging and see what we can find in this passage.

Whose good does God work for?

The verse tells us He is actively working for the good of those who love Him, who are "called according to His purpose." This means believers. If we are saved, we can know and be confident that God is working for our good. This does not imply He is against non-believers. It simply does not deal with them.

In how many things does God work for our good?

All! If you look up the word "all" in Greek, it has an incredible meaning that really gives us deep insight. It means... all.

"Ok, I get it," you say. Yet think about this. God is working for our good even when we have a bad day. He is acting for our benefit when we are in the middle of trials. There is no "except" or "but" attached to this promise. It is not negated during natural disasters, terrorist attacks, or personal trauma. If those things are not included in "all," we have a problem. Here's the catch. God is the one who decides what is good, not us.

Later as perspective sets in, we look back on that tough time and say with nostalgia that it was good.

How often do we find ourselves in the midst of a challenge or difficulty, and begin asking God to remove us from the situation? "Please take this away," we cry. However, God does not. We endure, we persevere, and we live through the situation. Later as perspective sets in, we look back on that tough time and say with nostalgia that it was good. We learned things, and we grew. God has worked good in our lives through a difficulty. What if He had answered our prayer to remove the hardship? We would have never experienced the good He intended for us.

I experienced this kind of "good" early in my marriage. My wife, Lindsey, was required to testify in a murder trial. The man on trial was her former youth pastor who was accused of murdering his wife and having multiple affairs with women in the congregation. It was perhaps the most difficult thing Lindsey had ever gone through in her life. I was certainly praying for God to remove this difficulty. It was not something I had dreamed of during the romantic first few months of marriage. Yet, rather than take it away, He gave us the strength to endure and go through that difficulty.

It turned out that she needed to testify against him at the murder trial. He ended up being convicted of killing his wife. It took years for Lindsey to walk through the pain of betrayal. Recently, I spent some time looking back on that period of our lives. I was able to see tremendous growth in my wife, as well as many of the women who were also involved. I was overcome by the tremendous amount of grace God showed the people involved in the tragedy. The growth and grace experienced came from walking through the difficult experience, not avoiding it.

As we look at events from God's perspective, we see an entirely different picture. Rather than being disconnected from difficult events, God is actively working in them, or in spite of them, to bring good to those who love him. It doesn't answer the difficult questions, but it does give us an unchangeable promise to cling to as we navigate life on a planet that is broken and corrupted by sin.

The wisdom of Ecclesiastes 7:14 says it well, "In the day of prosperity be joyful, and in the day of adversity consider:

God has made the one as well as the other, so that man may not find out anything that will be after him."

It is easy to be happy when times are good. True growth and trust in the character of God gives us peace during the days that bring adversity.

O: OMNIS – THE "ALLS" OF THE ALMIGHTY

O stands for the Omni's. These are the characteristics that separate God from man, the very things that give him the Capital "G" in front of his name. Omni is a prefix meaning "all." The first of these is Omniscient, or "all knowing." I could list pages and pages of passages that relate to this attribute, but here are a few:

"Sheol and Abaddon (some translations say "death and destruction") lie open before the Lord; how much more the hearts of the children of man" (Proverbs 15:11).

"I am God, and there is none like me, declaring the end from the beginning and from ancient times things not yet done, saying, My counsel shall stand, and I will accomplish all my purpose" (Isaiah 46:9b-10).

If God knows death and destruction, of course He knows the hearts of men. We count on this fact when we seek Him for direction. Imagine how disheartening would it be to hear God respond, "Hmm...I don't know!" When we seek God for guidance, we do so with confidence in His Omniscience. The spiritual gifts in 1 Corinthians 14 such as prophecy, words of knowledge, and wisdom rely on an all knowing God.

Today, this doctrine is under attack in the church. People will question, "How can God know the future and man still have free choice?" "Wouldn't this make us robots?" Logical explanations are employed in attempt to explain the mystery, things such as "God knows all things knowable." These explanations can seem to make rational sense to our finite minds. However, God is not like us. He is not finite or limited, but rather infinite. He cannot be contained by the human intellect. I will not attempt to explain how these things work together. It is not possible. We don't know how free will and God's omniscience work together, just that they are both true. We cannot change God. Truth causes us to adjust our questions. Scripture is clear: God knows all.

The second O or Omni, is that God is Omnipotent, or "all powerful." Sometimes in theological circles, this is referred to as sovereignty. A few of the passages referring to this are as follows:

"I know that you can do all things, and that no purpose of yours can be thwarted" (Job 42:2).

"Our God is in the heavens; he does all that he pleases" (Psalm 115:3).

Simply put, God can do whatever He wishes. If you couple this with the understanding that God is good, you come to an amazing realization: a perfectly good God, working for us, can steer anything that life throws at us towards a good result. No obstacle is too big! That is a God worthy of our worship!

The third and final O, is that God is Omnipresent. Simply, He is everywhere all the time. Several Scripture passages support this view:

"Where shall I go from your Spirit? Or where shall I flee from your presence? If I ascend to heaven, you are there! If I make my bed in Sheol, you are there! If I take the wings of the morning and dwell in the uttermost parts of the sea, even there your hand shall lead me, and your right hand shall hold me. If I say, Surely the darkness shall cover me, and the light about me be night, even the darkness is not dark to you; the night is bright as the day, for darkness is as light with you" (Psalm 139:7-12).

◎ ◉ ◎

God is not like us. He is not finite or limited, but rather infinite. He cannot be contained by the human intellect.

"Can a man hide himself in secret places so that I cannot see him? declares the Lord. Do I not fill heaven and earth? declares the Lord" (Jeremiah. 23:24).

What if the presence of God moved from country to country? We would enter into our time of prayers and petitions with the "30 percent chance of God's presence!" Thankfully, this is not true. God is more reliable than our local weather report! When I take a part of international prayer days where people are praying for the same thing all across the globe, I realize just how small we are. Knowing the Spirit of God is present throughout the world only enlarges my view of God.

D. DIVINE

The final part of our acronym is the most simple. The D in G-O-D represents Divine. Quite simply, He is God, and we are not. This sounds basic, but I find many theological viewpoints boil down to making God fit into our boxes. A good friend of mine once said, "Any God that can fit inside your head is too small." It was a memorable way to state the immensity of the God we serve.

TENSION AND MYSTERY

God doesn't mind tension. We are the ones who have such a hard time accepting it. God is full of things that seem to contradict, like the fact that He is fully loving and yet fully just. As humans, we cannot walk in perfect love and perfect justice simultaneously. How could we comprehend a God who can? Or that a God who can give people freedom of choice, yet still claim to know all things and be all powerful? In a finite creature, this would be impossible, yet God is infinite.

Something within us cannot deal with tension. Yet, God is perfectly comfortable with it. We want to choose sides, to affirm one aspect while denying another. Some even go so far as to change God to make Him fit with our understanding. "Surely there must be a logical, rational explanation," we say. Yet even our logic and powers of reason are finite. God, being God, can have two attributes that appear to contrast, yet are in perfect harmony.

Was this ever better illustrated than by Jesus, who was God, coming to earth as a flesh and blood man? Jesus was an all-knowing, all-powerful babe in the manger. He was God but with human feelings, emotions, and temptations. How could this be? It is a mystery. This is yet another illustration of the incomprehensible divine tension.

Charles Spurgeon once likened these attributes, that seem to contradict, to two sets of railroad tracks running side by side. Clearly they are separate and individual; yet, as you look in the distance they seem to become one. Now try as you might, you will never get to the place where they meet, although they appear to. God is like these railroad tracks. We cannot figure out how things fit together, but somehow, "in the distance" they do. The tension keeps us at a place of trust and reliance on a God who is bigger than us.

Paul himself illustrates this tension in the book of Romans. If you compare chapters 9 and 10, it can appear as if Paul represents two different theologies. Chapter 9 portrays God as an all powerful, sovereign Creator, saying strong statements such as, "But who are you, O man, to answer back to God? Will what is molded say to its molder, Why have you made me like this?" (Romans 9:21). God can do anything He wants, and a branch in theology known as Calvinism has taken this position, historically. It prompts jokes such as, "What did the Calvinist say after he fell down the stairs? Well, glad that is over with!" Such a view can lead to predetermination or even laziness (the future is set, so why bother). I know people who question the value of prayer due to an overzealous view of God's sovereignty.

Only one chapter later, Paul presents the other side of the coin. Romans 10 is a chapter highlighting how God gives man free will and various choices.

"For everyone who calls on the name of the Lord will be saved. But how are they to call on him in whom they have not believed? And how are they to believe in him of whom they have never heard? And how are they to hear without someone preaching? And how are they to preach unless they are sent? As it is written, How beautiful are the feet of those who preach the good news!" (Romans 10:13-15).

Here is the great mystery: God, though all powerful, uses man to help accomplish His purposes.

We must go out and share our faith. Our choices do matter and they have real consequences.

This view lines with the Arminian theological point of view. A zealous Arminian would say everything is up to you, that the future of the world hangs in the balance of your choices today.

⊚ ⊚ ⊚

God, being God, can have two attributes that appear to contrast, yet are in perfect harmony.

Yet right here in Romans, we see Paul affirms both views as true. He makes no attempt to reconcile these two attributes of God. Paul is comfortable with this Divine tension. Are we?

That is why I don't really like the terms Calvinist or Arminian. I prefer a third. Let's start a new group called Calminianists. This new group can affirm both the sovereignty of God and man's free will. Let's not serve a God of either, but one of both.

We will never totally figure out how all the mysteries of God work. Difficulties in Scripture or about God can be explained, but mysteries are what make God... well God. We could even say, "God with a capital G!" It is what makes Him different from us. It is why we worship Him.

Flannery O'Connor, an American writer in the mid 20th century, says it this way, "Whatever you do anyway, remember that these are mysteries and that if they were such that we could understand them, they wouldn't be worth understanding. A God you can understand would be less than yourself."

Our job is to pursue knowing Him, to ask the hard questions, to wrestle with the mysteries, all the while knowing the tension we feel is one specifically put there to keep us trusting in something greater than ourselves. Tension and mystery are two of the very things that cause me to worship God. I love the parts of God I don't under-stand. It gives me something tangible to look forward to in heaven. When I picture heaven, I don't imagine myself floating on a cloud singing worship songs. Instead, I picture an eternity of God revealing himself to us and answering our questions. Throw in some good coffee, and that sounds like heaven. Ah!

Is God ALWAYS the Good Guy?

Many of these attributes of God are easy to believe when things are going our way, when our wallets are full, and our bodies are healthy. The true test of trust does not come in the good times but in the difficult times. Anyone can have faith when life is good. The test comes when life feels broken.

Acts 12 starts off with a short account detailing the state of the church. They were only a few years removed from Jesus' death and resurrection. The church had the amazing experience of being filled with the Spirit at Pentecost in Acts 2, followed by thousands of people getting saved. Then, a bit removed from that emotional high, the reality of the cost of their beliefs set in. Persecution was happening:

> About that time Herod the king laid violent hands on some who belonged to the church. He killed James the brother of John with the sword, and when he saw that it pleased the Jews, he proceeded to arrest Peter also. This was during the days of Unleavened Bread. And when he had seized him, he put him in prison, delivering him over to four squads of soldiers to guard him, intending after the Passover to bring him out to the people. So Peter was kept in prison, but earnest prayer for him was made to God by the church" (Acts 12:1-5).

This passage highlights James and Peter who were the first-century equivalent of pastors of this young flock. One of their pastors was arrested and killed, the other co-pastor now finds himself in prison. You can imagine the strain upon this young church. Verse five tells us the believers earnestly prayed for Peter to be released. Imagine yourself in this prayer meeting. I don't think people would be falling asleep or feeling bored. The future of the church was at stake:

> Now when Herod was about to bring him out, on that very night, Peter was sleeping between two soldiers, bound with two chains, and sentries before the door were guarding the prison. And behold, an angel of the Lord stood next to him, and a light shone in the cell. He struck Peter on the side and woke him, saying, "Get up quickly". And the chains fell off his hands. And the angel said to him, Dress yourself and put on your sandals. And he did so. And he said to him, Wrap your cloak around you and follow me. And he went out and followed him. He did not know that what was being done by the angel was real, but thought he was seeing a vision. When they had passed the first and the second guard, they came to the iron gate leading into the city. It opened for them of its own accord, and they went out and went along one street, and immediately the angel left him. When Peter came to himself, he said, Now I am sure that the Lord has sent his angel and rescued me from the hand of Herod and from all that the Jewish people were expecting. When he realized

this, he went to the house of Mary, the mother of John whose other name was Mark, where many were gathered together and were praying. And when he knocked at the door of the gateway, a servant girl named Rhoda came to answer. Recognizing Peter's voice, in her joy she did not open the gate but ran in and reported that Peter was standing at the gate. They said to her, You are out of your mind. But she kept insisting that it was so, and they kept saying, It is his angel! But Peter continued knocking, and when they opened, they saw him and were amazed" (Acts 12:6-16).

What an amazing story! While the church is praying for Peter's release, God answers their prayers. Chains fall off wrists, guards are blinded, and city gates open of their own accord. Then to cap it off, Peter shows up at this very prayer meeting!

Can you picture the scene when Peter walks in the door? The place must have erupted!

Disciples jumping up and down, slapping Peter on the back.

Wives crying.

Saints rejoicing.

Imagine the feelings of Peter's wife as her husband walks through that door safe and sound! This is a prayer group I would like to be a part of!

This early church would have had no doubt the God they serve is good. They would be confident of His omniscience and His omnipresence, and would worship Him for his omnipotence. They have heard of huge city gates opening on their own. The church knew God was present with Peter in prison and in the prayer meeting at the same time. They witnessed his attention to the details of reminding Peter not to forget his cloak (vs 8).

God truly is mighty! I can imagine they had a fantastic worship service after this event.

However, there was one person in the room who may have had a different experience. In the midst of this miraculous deliverance, we are not told how one lone individual must have felt.

What of James's wife?

Surely she was happy for Peter. I can only guess she threw her arms around Mrs. Peter in celebration. After the excitement and worship died down, surely she had to think that difficult thought.

"Why not James?"

I think it is safe to assume the church also prayed when James was put in prison, but instead of being saved like Peter, he was killed.

Did God forget to be good?

Did he take a vacation from his Omni's?

Was it church's fault for not to praying hard and long enough?

God still was God, with a capital G, but the outcome was different.

Why?

We may speculate that it was James' time to go, that God knew he was finished. Perhaps it was the Enemy or just a result of life lived on a fallen planet. There is no perfect answer. There is no answer that will lessen the grief of a new widow.

THE RIGHT ATTITUDE

So what is our attitude to be?

In the book of Daniel Shadrack, Meshach, and Abednego are having their lives threatened by King Nebuchadnezzar who wanted them to worship the statue he made in his image. Daniel 3:15-18 says:

> Now if you are ready when you hear the sound of the horn, pipe, lyre, trigon, harp, bagpipe, and every kind of music, to fall down and worship the image that I have made, well and good.
>
> But if you do not worship, you shall immediately be cast into a burning fiery furnace. And who is the god who will deliver you out of my hands? Shadrach, Meshach, and Abednego answered and said to the king, O Nebuchadnezzar, we have no need to answer you in this matter. If this be so,

our God whom we serve is able to deliver us from the burning fiery furnace, and he will deliver us out of your hand, O king. But if not, be it known to you, O king, that we will not serve your gods or worship the golden image that you have set up.

Their response is telling. They acknowledge God is able to deliver them, but even if He doesn't, they will continue to worship God. The faith of these three men is not based on the outcome. Even in the face of death, they will not compromise their trust in God. Think of this story as you pray for friends to be healed of cancer or for your wallet to be a bit fuller. We pray with faith, but our faith is in the Healer and the Provider, not the physical result. On this side of heaven, some diseases will go uncured, some needs unmet. If our faith is in the outcome, we will be tossed to and fro, looking for the next "feel good" experience. But, our faith is in a God, who never changes.

> The faith of these three men is not based on the outcome.

This brings peace and stability to our lives. I once found an advertisement with Michael J. Fox on it. He is an actor from Back to the Future, Spin City, or for the older ones among us, Family Ties. Fox has Parkinson's disease, a condition that affects the nervous system and for which there is no cure. The first line of the ad caught my attention.

"Maybe I was supposed to get Parkinson's."

The ad went on to make a plea for funding research into finding a cure for this disease. If he could help find a cure, he would get a sense of meaning for his horrible disease. To my knowledge, Michael J. Fox is not a believer. Yet, he demonstrates a Godly response to this tragedy. How much more should we walk in a godly way in the face of difficulties?

We serve the God who makes good out of all things. Surely we can find the ability to endure the hardships life brings us.

The Biblical writers did not learn grace from a textbook or in a classroom. They learned it from the school of hardship and difficulty. They experienced the sufficiency of grace in the moment.

Daniel was thrown into the lion's den.

David hid in a cave fearing for his life.

Job lost everything, and his friends advised to curse God and die.

Paul himself was shipwrecked, stoned, and suffered under the ever present thorn in his flesh.

These are the same writers who teach us of God's goodness. Their bad days or difficult experiences did not change the character of God; it changed them. They never attempt to answer all the questions. They ask different ones.

On one of my first mission trips in my early twenties, I led a youth group to Poland. On one of our "off" days, we went to the former concentration camp at Auschwitz where thousands of Jews were executed during World War II. We toured the facility, walking through entire rooms of shoes, luggage, even human hair. We saw the cells that held captives, the posts where Jews were tied for firing squads, even the gas chambers. The experience left us all feeling heavy. It felt like getting hit by a bus. It was a very quiet ride back to our camp.

The same evening, we were scheduled to have a worship service with a local youth group.

Around a camp fire, we began half heartedly singing praise songs, still heavy from our experiences of the day. As we stood around the fire, people shared their testimonies. Soon, an elderly woman, the caretaker of the camp, stepped forward. Her first sentence had us sitting at the edges of our seats. "I was a prisoner at Auschwitz," she said.

The caretaker told us how she was imprisoned and knew she would be killed. The guards told her the next day would be her last. Weighed down, knowing she would face pain and be stripped of what little dignity she had left, the woman decided to take matters into her own hands. She broke rank, sprinting across the camp to throw herself on the electric fence and commit suicide. Normally, they would have shot her on sight, but somehow, she made it to the middle of the camp, where she met another woman also away from her group.

44

"What are you doing," said the stranger.

"I will die with dignity. I am going to kill myself," said the caretaker.

Right in the middle of Auschwitz, the strange woman shared the gospel, the message of hope, and in the middle of hell on earth, the caretaker believed, praying to accept Christ. As she finished and opened her eyes, she found she was alone. The other woman had vanished into thin air.

The caretaker headed back to the barracks with a peace in her heart. She was ready to face whatever came her way. She awoke the next morning to the sound of sirens. Running outside, she learned the war was over. She was free.

◎ ⊙ ◎

Their bad days or difficult experiences did not change the character of God; it changed them.

As she told us this story around the fire, shivers went down my spine. We had been at Auschwitz that very morning. Standing before us was a living testimony that God can make good even out of the worst humanity has to offer. Fifteen years later, I remember the moment like it was yesterday.

We can trust Him. On a good day or a bad day, through victory or trial, peace comes in the unchanging character of God. This must be foundational in our lives. We truly have security because of who God is and what He has done for us, not our circumstances. It was this assurance that enabled the early church to move on from the death of James and spread throughout the world.

I don't know about you, but I want a God who is active in my life. I want a Superhero! But, it doesn't have to be me!

I realize this can open up a can of worms. Believers go through unspeakable things. I know this all too well. I work in Africa where believers are regularly the victims of crime and abuse. However, I think believing these events are outside of God's domain is far scarier.

Consider the words of Jerry Bridges, President of the discipleship group, the Navigators. "If there is a single event in all the universe that can occur outside of God's sovereign control, then we cannot trust Him. God is never surprised, caught off guard, or frustrated by change."[4]

QUESTIONS
for discussion

Why do we need God to be the filter through which we view the world?

What difficulties or hindrances distract us from believing that God is always working for our good?

How can we walk in a faith based on the character of God, not one dependent on a certain outcome or result?

"I do not hesitate to say that those who examined my life would not see an extraordinary amount of sin, yet as I looked upon myself I saw outrageous sin against God. I was not like others, untruthful, dishonest, swearing, and so on. But all of a sudden, I met Moses carrying the law; the Ten Commandments...and as I read them, they all seemed to join in condemning me in the sight of Jehovah."

CHARLES SPURGEON

If Paying For Sin Were Up To Us...

If we were superheroes, sin would be our kryptonite. Just as this mysterious green rock renders Superman powerless, the power of sin continually weakens us. Sin lurks in the shadows, derailing all our good intentions. We think we can will our way to be a follower of Christ, but the more we strive, the more we fail.

Paul refers to this "tug of war" with his kryptonite in Romans 7:16-24:

> For I know that nothing good dwells in me, that is, in my flesh. For I have the desire to do what is right, but not the ability to carry it out. For I do

not do the good I want, but the evil I do not want is what I keep on doing. Now if I do what I do not want, it is no longer I who do it, but sin that dwells within me. So I find it to be a law that when I want to do right, evil lies close at hand. For I delight in the law of God, in my inner being, but I see in my members another law waging war against the law of my mind and making me captive to the law of sin that dwells in my members. Wretched man that I am!

If we see grace in its proper perspective, we will give up our exhausting superhero charade.

So why would I talk about sin in a book on grace? Grace is the solution to the problem of sin, and without a proper understanding of the problem, we will never fully grasp the magnitude of grace. If we see the corruption that sin has brought into our own lives and the entire planet, then, and only then, can we see the vastness of the gift of grace. If we see grace in its proper perspective, we will give up our exhausting superhero charade.

We will look at sin in a way that may be a bit new for some of you. We are going to look at sin through the eyes of the sacrificial system in the Old Testament. There are many parallels when you compare the

Old Testament Law with striving for good works as modern day believers.

In order to see these similarities, put yourself in the sandals of an Old Testament believer. The first thing you would have to internalize is that Jesus would not be there to rescue you.

You would, however, know that one day a Messiah would come to save you from your sin.This Messianic belief came from Genesis 3, just after Adam and Eve sinned. Prior to this act of disobedience, sin and death didn't exist, but ever since then, man has lived on a broken planet in need of fixing. The good news, for both us and the Old Testament believer, is that God's plan of redemption was launched just verses later in Genesis 3:15, "I will put enmity between you and the woman, and between your offspring and her offspring; he shall bruise your head, and you shall bruise his heel."

From your perspective as an Old Testament believer, you would have been told the offspring of Eve will be the Messiah and He will defeat sin and death. No more details are given than that, only the commands and sacrifices of the Law.

So come on a journey with me, a journey back in time, to the time of the Old Testament believer. Let's be the best Old Testament believers we can be!

THAT'S A LOT OF SHEEP!

In the Old Testament, sin was dealt with using a sacrificial system. There are countless situations and rules pertaining to these sacrifices, but some general principles remain the same. For the sake of illustration, we will focus on these common threads.

Imagine you have stolen someone's cloak, and you are racked by guilt and want to make it right. After returning the cloak, you would have to go through an elaborate procedure to make things right between you and God. First, you would have to go to your flock and pick out an animal to sacrifice. Your selfish nature might immediately look for the frailest animals you own. God, however, says you must give the best. It has to be a perfect sacrifice. The animal may not be injured in any way. It may not have a torn ear or even a spot on its skin. It must be a pure, spotless sacrifice. Since the economy of this period treated animals as currency, your sin would cost you financially. The source of food in your life came from your flock as well. Sin would even affect your waistline! It would be so much easier to go down the street to the sacrifice store and pick up a perfect lamb. God did not make it that easy. He made it costly.

You then take that perfect lamb down to the temple to present it to the priest. From our modern day perspective, Old Testament priests often get a bad reputation. They owned no land. They dealt with blood and guts all day long, and I imagine they would carry a certain stench with them.

Who would want to be a priest?

It can be easy to project all the messiness of the sacrifice on the priest as he does his job. The book of Leviticus tells us the reverse is true. When you present a perfect lamb to the priest as an offering for the sin of stealing, first you would confess your sin. You, the sinner, place your hand on the head of that sweet little lamb. You speak out your sin over the animal symbolizing the transferring of sin from you to the animal. Then, as you hold your hand on the head of that cuddly, soft lamb, you use the other hand to slit the animal's throat. The lamb chokes on its own blood as the priest collects some in a bowl. The animal bleeds to death while you continue to hold your hand on its head.

That lamb came to the temple an innocent, little, grass-munching animal.

What changed?

Sin.

Sin caused this animal to die. Until there was sin on the animal, it was fine. Your sin killed this lamb. Your dirty work is not finished yet. After the animal is dead, you skin it, butchering the animal by removing all the organs. Then you cut the animal into pieces.

Who has the messy job?

The priest collects the blood, arranges wood for the fire, places the meat on the altar, and burns the sacrifice, throwing the collected blood on the altar in the process.

Everything to do with killing, skinning, and butchering the animal is the responsibility of the sinner. Sin is both costly and messy.

◉ ◉ ◉

The principle for an Old Testament believer is one sin equals one sacrifice.

Once you have completed this entire process, the priest, empowered by God, forgives you for stealing your neighbor's cloak.

One sin.

If you commit three sins, how many sacrifices are required?

Three. The principle for an Old Testament believer is one sin equals one sacrifice.

Another truth the sacrificial system reveals to us is the standard God uses in dealing with sins. How many sins in our lives that are NOT sacrificed for does it take to be declared guilty as a sinner?

Just one.

Even if we sacrifice 100 times, if we miss one sin, we are a sinner. The standard of God when dealing with sin is perfection. We cannot miss a single sin!

So already we see three things: First is that sin is costly. Second, every sin requires a sacrifice. Finally, there is not a giant scale in heaven weighing out bad sins and worse sins. All sin must be dealt with the same.

As you put yourself in the place of an Old Testament believer how do you feel? Where is your confidence level in keeping what is required of a good believer in the Old Testament? You might wonder if you can do it. Will you have enough sheep?

You might wondering, if you have to sacrifice one spotless lamb for every sin you commit, how do you know what a sin is in the first place.

Ten Commandments

The Ten Commandments are God's "Top Ten List" on sin. In these commandments we find every kind of sin possible to commit. Let's first look at the forms sin can take. At first glance, the Ten Commandments looks like a list of actions, of things not to do. The list is as follows:

1. You shall have no other gods
2. Do not make any graven images (idols)
3. Do not misuse the name of the Lord
4. Honor the sabbath day
5. Honor your mother and father
6. Do not murder
7. Do not commit adultery
8. Do not steal

9. Do not bear false witness

10. Do not covet your neighbor's wife or possessions

We see sin can be a bad action such as adultery, murder, or stealing. A closer look at the list reveals sin can take the form of the words we speak as well. Bearing false witness pertains to our speech. So sin happens in our actions and speech. Anything else?

Where does the coveting command fit? Can we "act" or "say" coveting?

Coveting is an inward thought or desire of the heart.

Often when we study the teachings of Jesus, it seems as if He made the rules tougher. In Matthew 5:26-27 he says, "You have heard that it was said, 'You shall not commit adultery.' But, I say to you that everyone who looks at a woman with lustful intent has already committed adultery with her in his heart." He made a similar statement about anger in our heart being equal to murder. Is Jesus making this difficult?

He is correctly interpreting the Ten Commandments. Sin has always included both thoughts and desires.

As an Old Testament believer, you must be aware of all your actions, thoughts, words, and desires so that you can take care of all of your sins at the Temple.

As I put myself in these shoes, I think I would be a note-book-keeping saint. Somewhere in the folds of my robe, I would have a list. Going through my day, I would jot down my sins. Perhaps I could keep pace with my actions or on good days my words. The difficult thing would be to acknowledge every sinful thought that crosses my mind.

Imagine a typical morning. You grumpily roll out of bed, and your thoughts fall far short of gratitude for the new day God gave you. Staggering down the hall, you step on a child's toy. A curse word springs to your minds, or even comes out your mouth. Upon entering the kitchen, you see the milk your spouse left on the counter overnight. With thoughts of judgment and criticism flooding your mind, you boil water for your coffee. Consumed with criticism, the water overflows, burning your fingers as you yank the kettle off the burner. With anger continuing to boil over, you slam the kettle down into the sink. Finally, after recovering enough to make your coffee, you settle into a chair for our spiritual time with God.

How many sinful words and thoughts did the preceding episode include? How many sacrifices would need to be made if we were Old Testament saints? What about sinful desires? Do I even know each one? However, like a good Old Testament saint, you get out your list and start jotting down your sins so you can follow the plan that God has laid out for your forgiveness.

Just for the sake of illustration, let's spend a bit of time looking even closer at the Ten Commandments. As an Old Testament believer, we would need to know exactly what sin is, so if we committed it, we can make it right through the sacrificial system. As you go through these commands, think about how many you have broken. Perhaps you might even like to keep a tally in the margins or on a separate sheet of paper to see what it feels like to keep track of your sins and pay for them in your own strength. Don't worry about how many times you have committed the sin (although the true Law would demand payment for quantity as well). If you have ever committed the sin, make a note or mark on the page. As you make each tally, imagine your hand on the head of a fresh lamb.

1. YOU SHALL HAVE NO OTHER GODS

The first commandment challenges you to commit to God as the Source and only Truth. All the other commandments assume understanding of this first one.

God gave Israel these commandments after He had demonstrated his superiority over the gods of Egypt. When God sent plagues on Pharaoh and Egypt recorded for us in the book of Exodus, He sent things that related to the various Egyptian gods. He took these pagan gods on and demonstrated himself as superior.

If you have ever worshiped another god in your life besides the One who warrants the capital G, mark your paper and imagine yourself preparing to make a sacrifice. This would include any religion or worldview that does not acknowledge the One and Only God as the Truth.

2. Do not make any graven images (idols)

An idol is an image or representation of either a god or something we value. God demands that we do not worship any idols or images because none can represent how huge He is. While Old Testament believers would have considered idols to be little statues and images of gods, they can also be anything in our lives that replace God. People, such as leaders, spouses, or even churches, can be idols as well as possessions, money, and careers. If we find ourselves unwilling to give any of these things up in order to obey God, it is likely they possess the top spot God desires.

In Bible School, we were given a few questions that put the idol commandment in perspective:

In a time of need, where do we turn for comfort or help?

When you feel bad, what do you want to do?

Are there any addictions in your life?

What do you allow to control your life?

I assume based on these questions that there are some marks being made in our little sin notebooks right now. Among other things, I made marks for running to false comforts when faced with difficult issues.

3. Do not misuse the name of the Lord

The third commandment is often interpreted as saying the Lord's name as a swear word. While I would say this is included in the command, misusing the name of God involves more than swearing.

How is it possible to commit this sin in action, word or desire?

This command is God telling us His name is valuable and worthy of honor. As ambassadors of this Name, we represent Him in everything we do, think, or say!

Have you ever misused the name of the Lord?

I've been personally challenged on this one when considering using the name of God attached to a word of knowledge. When I feel I have something to share with someone from God, I try to avoid saying, "God said." If my encouragement is from God, the person receiving it will know that without me having to tell them.

We can disobey this command if we attach God's name for weight or emphasis. If you are a leader, do you tell people "God told me this is what you are to do?" Perhaps you have heard the infamous, "God told me to marry you!" I could go on and on about the potentially damaging effects of this statement. We need the fear of the Lord to realize that we are fallible. Often we hear God correctly, but there are times when we miss it, and at its worst, this becomes manipulation. Thus, I would include all of these misuses of God's name in this commandment. (Don't forget to make those marks on your paper.)

4. Honor the Sabbath Day

If I write a second book, there is a good chance a large portion of it will be about the Sabbath. I could go on for many chapters, but will try to keep this brief.

This command is the most surprising of the list, the one modern believers often feel at liberty to disobey. The penalty in the Old Testament for breaking the Sabbath was death (Exodus 31:15). Really? Death for not taking a day off?

God modeled this commandment in Genesis when He rested on the seventh day, and some rabbis suggest He may have created rest, peace, and solitude itself on that seventh day.[5] Without getting into a two-hour sermon on the subject, the heart of the matter is one of trust. By honoring the

Sabbath, we declare that God is our source, that God will help us to do in six days what we believe we need seven for. If God is our reality, we can and should rest. God says it is sin if we do not because at its essence we would be declaring we do not trust in God as our source and sufficiency. Pencils all over the world are marking down this commandment on sin lists!

5. HONOR YOUR MOTHER AND FATHER

Ah, the Sunday school favorite (at least for the parents)!

Just as we honor the Sabbath to show honor to our heavenly source, this commandment directs us to honor our earthly source. Even the worst parents should be honored for providing life. When we honor our mothers and fathers, we honor also honor ourselves. When we value the source of our physical existence we esteem value to ourselves as well.

...at its essence we would be declaring we do not trust in God as our source and sufficiency.

If you broke this commandment in the period of the Old Testament, it also held the death penalty. There was no teenage rebellion phase in the Old Testament. The rebels would have been killed! God takes honor seriously.

The word "honor" does not mean showing blind obedience or pretending our parents were perfect. Honoring is related to the way we talk about our parents. Take a moment and consider your attitudes and the words you speak. Do we honor your parents through your words? If you haven't honored them in action, word, or attitude, make a mark on your sin list.

6. Do not murder

This commandment shows the value God places on life. However, as we have already explored, murder in the heart requires a sacrifice as well. You probably have not committed the act of murder, but you should make a mark on your paper if you have ever given a look, had a thought, and or held an attitude that could "kill." We have all experienced these "looks" from a family member or someone on the road that we just cut off as we drive our car, and if you've ever been on the other side of that look, go ahead and make your mark.

7. Do not commit adultery

This commandment is inclusive of sexual sin in each form: Action, word, or attitude. If you have ever had an impure thought, or even committed adultery in action, make your mark. When we break God's standard for an exclusive sexual relationship between one man and one woman in marriage, we sin. This is most often done in our thoughts. We call this lust. As an Old Testament believer this would require a sacrifice.

8. Do not steal

God values property. There is no monetary amount attached to this commandment. When we steal, even inexpensive things, the same sacrifice is required. Lying on your time card or even tax evasion would also require a sacrifice for the Old Testament believer.

9. Do not bear false witness

In Sunday School, we are taught one of the Ten Commandments is "thou shall not lie." This is not the case. Of course this commandment includes lying, but it also covers even more such as socially accepted sins of gossip, slander, or even silence when we should have spoken up.

10. Do not covet your neighbor's wife or possessions

As previously mentioned, this is where we move beyond the realm of action and into words and attitudes, attitudes such as envy, jealousy, and ungratefulness. If we disobey this commandment, at its core, we are telling God the Creator that He made a mistake, or even that he isn't able to give us good gifts at all. Yikes! I need to make lots of marks on my list.

The point I'm trying to make is that life as an Old Testament believer would feel like an overwhelming sense of failure and sinfulness. I assume many would wonder if it is even possible to keep such a standard. How about you? Since you are putting yourself in the place of an Old Testament believer, how do you feel?

Do You Have Enough Sheep?

When I teach this, my audience is often quite despondent at this point. They don't see much love, joy, or peace in this Old Testament salvation message. So I attempt to cheer them up by providing an opportunity for them to sacrifice for their sins. We don't head outside to begin slaughtering animals, though. Instead, I pass out a small bag of animal crackers (or biscuits) to each person.

Picture yourself with this "flock of animals." Now compare the number of sins on your checklist with the amount of animals in the bag. Since the number on our page is quite high, and the amount of whole animals in the baggie is small, the excitement of a mid-lecture snack usually dissipates quickly.

Notice I mentioned whole animals. Remember any animal with blemishes (e.g. broken cracker-legs) cannot be used for a sacrifice. These broken, gnarled animals can be eaten. These sheep can be enjoyed in a BBQ or a South African braai! But any whole animals must be reserved for sin sacrifices. You might experience a deep sense of emptiness in your stomach! Invariably, there are not enough whole sacrifices to go around.

The only solution is to be better in the future. If you don't commit any more sins, you won't lose any more sheep you don't have. You won't put yourself deeper into God's debt. To be a good Old Testament believer, now you must be perfect.

Following this exercise, you will be in one of three camps.

> 1. After "sacrificing" your unblemished crackers, you might still have a few whole animal crackers remaining. Congratulations, you live to sin another day! But before you get too proud, let's be honest. You would be required to sacrifice for

quantity as well. Not one sacrifice for lying, but one for every lie over the course of your life.

2. Others might be perfectly even. Ten sins. Ten sacrifices with no room to spare. You are totally forgiven, but you need to live a perfect life from now on. Good luck with that!

3. The third and most common group are the ones who give all they have, but it is not enough to erase the list. This might leave you feeling depressed and ready to quit.

Now, you're probably wondering, why would you even bother trying to do this? Surely God looks at the heart! Right?

God says if there is even one sin, it breaks the entire covenant. Leviticus 26:14-15 tells us, "But if you will not listen to me and will not do all these commandments, if you spurn my statutes, and if your soul abhors my rules, so that you will not do all my commandments, but break my covenant, then I will do this to you..." This passage is followed by a huge list of covenant curses. This means that one mistake is the same as a million. One mistake breaks the entire covenant the same as if you broke every command in the Law continuously. With God's standard of perfection, you are no closer to a right relationship with God than you were when you had more food and animals. You are either holy or a sinner, there is no in between. If God looks at your heart, it will be deemed wicked and the wages will be death.

When I was in school, I brought home one particular report card I still remember. I received all A's but one. I received a B in math. In an attempt to motivate me to do my best, my parents pointed out the one B. Our sin list is a little like that. We have to get straight A's or we're not good enough. Even one B corrupts an otherwise perfect report card.

We say, "Surely God will look at the heart," but knowing His standard is perfection, do we really want God to look at our hearts? This isn't karma. God does not measure our good deeds against the bad ones. God's standard requires perfection. Even one sin that is not paid for, requires punishment and justice. Romans 6:23 tells us, "the wages of sin is death".

Things are not looking good for any Old Testament believer. Many would have quit by this point. Isn't there something in the Old Testament that talks of all sins being forgiven?

DAY OF ATONEMENT

In Leviticus 16, there is a celebration that occurs once a year among the people of God in the Old Testament. The Day of

Atonement is a festival in which the entire nation assembles from morning till night, confessing their sins to God. Near the end of the day two goats are brought to the high priest. The high priest takes the first goat and places his hand on its head. As with the sin sacrifice, this symbolically transfers sin onto that goat, only this was the sin of the whole nation. This goat was sacrificed for the sin of the people. The priest then takes a second goat, repeating the symbolism. This goat is not killed, but instead, the whole people of Israel drive out the goat into the barren places.

This goat is known as the scapegoat. Symbolically, the sin of the nation is driven away, never to be seen again. The people are clean! They erupt into a huge celebration. They are forgiven, what a relief! This celebration takes place once a year.

There is a dark side to this story. Old Testament believers would wake up the next morning and go back to one sacrifice for every sin. Once a year, they experienced complete freedom. The other 364 days were business as usual. I think I would pray to die on the Day of Atonement so I could make it to heaven!

How Did Anyone Get Saved?

The basic question here is, "Why did God give His people an impossible standard?"

Perhaps He is the angry God we often perceive in the pages of the Old Testament. If you're still following our exercise to be the best Old Testament believer possible, by this point you would be hopeless, unable to keep up with the requirements of the Law. You are likely at the point of frustration, even utter desperation. It is at this point we throw up our hands and say, "Help! I need someone to rescue me!"

Who is our superhero?

> It is at this point we throw up our hands and say, "Help! I need someone to rescue me!"

Remember, we have an idea as Old Testament believers that the Messiah is coming someday to rescue us. But who is that Messiah?

The answer is Jesus. In the New Testament, we place our faith in Christ for salvation. We believe in the life, death, and resurrection of Jesus that occurred in the past. However, for an Old Testament believer to place their faith in Christ, there is only one problem: the timeline.

An Old Testament believer looks forward to the first coming of the Messiah by faith, the same way we look back.

Let me ask you this. How many of you believe that one day there will be a second coming of Christ?

All of us do. We do not know all the details or the order of events, but we place our faith in that which we do know. The same way we believe in the future event of the second coming is how an Old Testament believer looked forward to the future event of the first coming. The source of salvation is always Christ.

Old Testament saints like Moses, Joshua, and David got this idea. If they did not, we would have a record of them trying to keep the Law and literally camping out at the temple day after day, making sacrifices for their sins. Instead, we see them offering an occasional sacrifice, most often in the context of worship. They understood that being right with God was an issue of faith, not of works or sacrifices.

God, who is not contained by time and space, is able to say Christ's work on the cross is always "now." This is consistent with the name given to Moses of God in Exodus 3:14. I AM. God is yesterday, today, and forever. There is nowhere you can go in time to escape God's presence. Salvation for an Old Testament saint or for the 21st century believer reading these pages, is found in the same source. Jesus. He is our superhero.

What good is the Old Testament Law then?

The Law still has value. It reveals the character of God. It shows what sin is and the cost it brings. The Law also gives wisdom. Let's leave the Old Testament believer's head and return to the present. The Law gives us modern day believers principles to live by, too. No one will ever keep the Law perfectly, but we can set this standard before us. When we move towards it, we grow closer to God in the process.

It's similar to what we say about holiness or living a godly lifestyle. We will never measure up perfectly, but if we live based on God's principles; we walk in wisdom. As a result, we grow closer to God. Holiness does not save, nor does the Law. The only salvation in all of history is Christ and His sacrifice on the cross.

We are no longer Old Testament believers. We can now bring back Jesus and breathe a "sigh of relief." But, do not put away your animal crackers just yet. We will return to this illustration throughout the rest of the book.

The frustration experienced in this exercise represents a life lived based on works. Your best is not enough. Even if God looks at your heart, you're in trouble. God requires perfection, and in these pages we will see how we can achieve that through Christ. Many believers today can relate to this in their faith. You might be frustrated that you can't stop sinning, discouraged about the impossibility of perfection, even close to giving up your faith.

"The rules are too difficult," you might say.

However, this was never the intention of Christianity. God designed a system causing a man who attempts to measure up to God's standard in his own strength to FAIL. In essence, God gave man an impossible standard to live up to so we would need Him. Not only need Him, but God wants us to be desperate for Him!

The good news is that the moment we cry for help, He is waiting with a gift. This is indescribable. It is the gift of salvation. Now we get to explore this gift, which is the solution to the sin problem.

Questions
for discussion

What emotions did you experience during the animal cracker exercise? Have you ever experienced any similar emotions in your relationship with God?

In your own words, describe the difference between being saved by faith and making holiness your goal and focus.

"The world can do almost anything as well or better than the church. You need not be a Christian to build houses, feed the hungry, or heal the sick. There is only one thing the world cannot do. It cannot offer grace."

GORDON MACDONALD

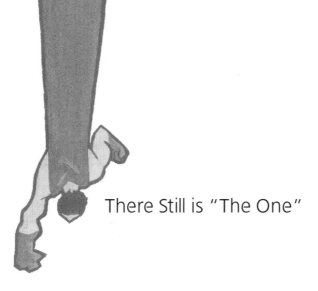

There Still is "The One"

In movies and television shows there is often an idea of "the one." In the Matrix trilogy of films, Neo was "the one" to save the world from the machines. The television show, Lost, was always in search of the one person to lead the people off the island. Another classic example is Luke Skywalker, who was the only one able to resist the lure of the dark side and save the universe!

Some of the best stories man has dreamt up involve the concept "the one". A superhero. A Savior. Unfortunately, we are often misguided by the notion that we need to be the superhero, that we must save our own planet. Fortunately THE ONE has already come.

At this point we will begin to bridge the gap from the Old Testament to the New. We covered the problem of sin. Now we move to the solution, and there is no better place to begin our transition than the book of Hebrews. Written to a Jewish audience, the author sought to demonstrate how Christ is superior to all the elements of Jewish history and religion. Chapter 10:11-14 says, "And every priest stands daily at his service, offering repeatedly the same sacrifices, which can never take away sins. But when Christ had offered for all time a single sacrifice for sins, he sat down at the right hand of God, waiting from that time until his enemies should be made a footstool for his feet. For by a single offering he has perfected for all time those who are being sanctified."

In the Old Testament, the priests continually offered sacrifices but never fully dealt with the problem of sin. But when Christ comes, there is a huge change! Christ offers one sacrifice, for all time, for all sin. Then He sits down.

Why does Jesus sit down? Do you think he was tired or a bit worn out?

No, the work was finished. There was nothing more that needed to be done. A priest in the Old Testament would never sit down as there were always more sacrifices to make. Christ's work stands in contrast to a priest's perpetual working. His work is complete.

As a person crying out for a Messiah, we receive this sacrifice covering all sin for all time. We call this getting saved or being "born again."

It's Not Fair

Is the idea that all humankind inherited one man's sin as preposterous as it sounds?

It would be as if an innocent man served the sentence of a known felon. He didn't commit the crime, so why would he serve the time? The thought of being responsible for someone else's sin just doesn't seem fair.

The apostle Paul talks about this idea in Romans 5:12, "Therefore, just as sin came into the world through one man, and death through sin, and so death spread to all men because all sinned."

I often tell my children, "You should know better." It really is humorous if you stop and consider what I have just said. Children don't know better; they are children. In the same way, we think humans have the ability to "know better." This is equally as humorous. Adam and Eve were told to obey one command, and they were unable to do it. What possesses us to think we can do what we know we should? Paul would say our humanity or flesh is more inclined to sin than it is to "know better."

The source of this inclination to sin was Adam, the sinner, who ate the fruit in the Garden of Eden. He committed the first sin and as a punishment he was the first man to die. All of humankind after him will suffer this fate. Paul states, "all have sinned." This is the sin of Adam, which was passed to each and every human who followed. We didn't commit the act in the Garden, yet are still born into sin. He goes on to state in verse 16 that "condemnation and judgment" will be the products of sin. Not only are you born into sin, but you have to pay for it. The destiny of a person in Adam is both judgment and condemnation, in other words, hell! There is no way this is fair or just!

⊚ ⊙ ⊚

It is truly unfair that believers are blessed with so many amazing gifts as a part of their salvation. These are gifts of God's unmerited favor. In other words: grace.

As we look at the entire passage in its context, we see Paul is making a contrast. He is comparing Adam and the results of his actions with the actions of Christ. In Romans 5:15-16, he says, "But the free gift is not like the trespass. For if many died through one man's trespass, much more have the grace of God and the free gift by the grace of that one man Jesus Christ abounded for many. And the free gift is not like the result of that one man's sin. For the judgment following one trespass brought condemnation, but the free gift following many trespasses brought justification."

Paul brings Christ into a direct contrast to Adam. The only way for people to change their citizenship as a member of Adam to a member of Christ is to believe and be saved. When that occurs, they receive the free gift of justification

78

and grace. Their final destiny has been changed from hell to heaven.

Let me ask you this question, why do we cry about inheriting Adam's sin as unfair, but not about receiving the blessings of Christ as being unfair? If we look at this through the filter of fairness, neither one is fair. In each case, we are receiving an outcome we did nothing to deserve. Let's be honest. If fairness is the way we evaluate this, it is less fair to get righteousness (verse 19), justification, and grace for merely exercising faith. It would be more fair for us to be punished and receive the things Adam brings. The argument of being unfair does not stand the test. It is truly unfair that believers are blessed with so many amazing gifts as a part of their salvation. These are gifts of God's unmerited favor. In other words: grace.

The next time we are tempted to think people being born into sin is unfair, let us remind ourselves that the true injustice was that God would give us a gift so undeserved. Let's be motivated to tell people about the gift rather than shaking our fists at God telling Him that His ways are unfair. Salvation is never about fairness.

Two Groups

As the passage in Romans 5 illustrates, there are only two groups of people that Scripture is concerned about: those who believe and those who don't. We often separate people by sex, race, or nationality. The ultimate answer to racism, sexism, and national pride lies in these passages. God defines humanity differently. Galatians 3:28 tells us, "There is neither Jew nor Greek, there is neither slave nor free, there is neither male nor female, for you are all one in Christ Jesus." What an amazing statement of unity. If we are believers, we are one in Christ.

Scripture illustrates this unity in several different ways. Revelation gives us the clearest picture of these groups (Who would have thought!). In John's vision, we see the future of believers and unbelievers; one is a good future, and the other is not. Elsewhere, John calls them children of blessing and children of wrath. Colossians and Ephesians favor the titles of dead or alive. As we have seen, Paul calls the camps the sons of Adam and the sons of Christ. The only way to change your citizenship is to cry out to the great immigration officer in the sky for a Messiah.

When we do this, we receive amazing gifts Paul says accompany joining Christ's team, gifts such as righteousness, justification, and life. We will look more closely at these gifts later. We have spent a great deal of time on the problem of sin, but as promised, God's solution is up to the task. Salvation can handle the hugeness of sin with an enormity of its own! Frustration and despair can set in when we consider the magnitude of our sin. However, the gospel rescues us from this despair.

As we close this chapter and prepare to speak of our salvation, I am reminded of another quote from Jerry Bridges. In a sermon about how Christians can grow, Bridges offered a simple yet profound definition. He said, "Maturity as a Christian is about mastering the basics."

A professional athlete spends countless hours practicing the basic skills of his sport. Over and over, he perfects the basic skills required for his sport.

Do we do this in our Christian walk?

Or do we look to the latest interpretation of prophetic events or move of the Holy Spirit to come down, thinking this is the new secret to success?

In his book Outliers, Malcolm Gladwell estimates that becoming an expert in your field is not based on natural talent alone but on repeated practice of the essentials. Most experts, he says, invest 10,000 hours in their trade before they can be considered elite. God would have us invest time in mastering the simple yet life-transforming basics of our faith. It is to this place of maturity that our journey takes us next. 'The One" to save the world from sin is worth investing our time in.

QUESTIONS for discussion

We often look at God through our own grid of what we consider to be fair or just. Is it fair that God gives us the gift of salvation?

Discuss the quote of Jerry Bridges. "Maturity as a Christian is about mastering the basics." What are the basics of the Christian faith? How much time in your life do you devote to developing or meditating on these truths?

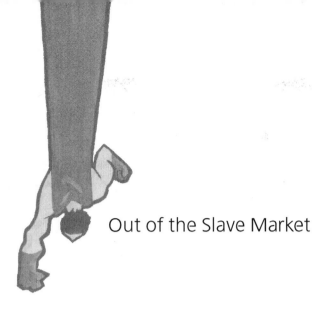

Out of the Slave Market

Do you ever feel like no matter how hard you try, you never can make it to the place where you can say with confidence God is pleased with you?

You strive to do all the right things, yet certain sins keep creeping up again and again. You may feel like one of those mice in the pet store who run on the wheel frantically, only to get tired without making it anywhere. Or else you're overwhelmed by mornings of screaming children and endless chores that seem to crowd out the possibility of any time with God. Do you look towards the sky wondering if the lightning bolt from God will strike you down for not spending time with Him?

Many of us can relate to these feelings. We find ourselves looking around church on a Sunday comparing our spiritual maturity with those around us. We do more than just admire someone's relationship with God; we compete to feel better about ourselves. Thoughts flood our minds like, "That guy is so much more spiritual than me. That girl is so much closer to God than I am." While there is nothing wrong with admiring people, it becomes wrong when we feel as if we are second-class citizens in God's kingdom.

Can you relate to these scenarios? If this resonates with you, you will want to meditate on Romans 3:21-26.

In his letter to the Romans, Paul is attempting to bring two groups of people together in unity. The church in Rome is made up of Jewish and Gentile believers. In the first century, reconciling these groups was the same as trying to mix oil and water. In 49 AD, the Jews were kicked out of Rome under the emperor, Claudius. This allowed the Gentiles to establish themselves as the church in Rome, bringing their culture and style to their worship services. Then, five years later in 54 AD, the Jews were allowed back in under Emperor Nero. Imagine the clash of cultures that came from two such different people groups. The Jews returned to town expecting everything to be the same as it was. They were shocked to find pagan, Gentile culture in the church. These two groups of people hated each other. They were the worst of enemies. This is the tension Paul writes into as he attempts to bring these two groups together.

84

Paul focuses on things they have in common rather than the obvious differences. He shows how everyone begins their journey as a sinner, both Jew and Gentile alike. Then he moves to discuss salvation itself, seeking to bring common ground to both groups. Just as both groups are sinners, both are now saved. Following this, he deals with life after salvation, elaborating on a new believer's journey of sanctification or holiness. Paul again shows all live and grow in the Christian life the same way; there is no distinction between Jew and Gentile.

Let's analyze how Paul builds unity between enemies by looking at the text in Romans 3:21-26:

> But now the righteousness of God has been manifested apart from the law, although the Law and the Prophets bear witness to it the righteousness of God through faith in Jesus Christ for all who believe. For there is no distinction: for all have sinned and fall short of the glory of God, and are justified by his grace as a gift, through the redemption that is in Christ Jesus, whom God put forward as a propitiation by his blood, to be received by faith. This was to show God's righteousness, because in his divine forbearance he had passed over former sins. It was to show his righteousness at the present time, so that he might be just and the justifier of the one who has faith in Jesus.

Simple right?

Clear...as mud!

There are some big words in this passage, words like righteousness, redemption, justified, and propitiation.

Propitiation?

Paul's writing style can be one that takes a bit of time to understand. Today we find ourselves singing these words in worship songs but often don't know what they mean. Very few of us have a clue about a word such as propitiation! To get a feel for what Paul is saying here, we need to take a deeper look at these ideas and concepts. The Bible can literally be Greek to us when we do not study what is being communicated to the original readers. Let's begin our journey by looking at the word redemption.

REDEMPTION – FROM SLAVERY TO FREEDOM

I have spent nearly 20 years working in missions, and I have met in my time, many people who serve with various motivations. Some serve out of a desire to help those pushed down by life and society. Some serve in order to fulfill part of the Great Commission. Others serve for the less noble motivation of travel.

Still, the ones who are the most miserable on the missions field are those serving out of a sense of guilt or obligation. They begin their commitments with zeal and passion. Then, things get tough. Culture shock hits. The converts don't come rolling in. When things go bad, those motivated by guilt often get depressed with the pain and suffering they see. Some feel guilty for being born into a Christian family or one that provided for their basic needs. Usually they give up and leave the field (or even their faith) completely. When we serve for the wrong reasons, the mission field will chew us up and spit us out.

I believe it begins with a wrong understanding of our salvation. As we talked about before, these people feel guilty for receiving the amazing gift of salvation. They feel they have to earn it through missions. However, if they really understood what redemption means, I believe they wouldn't be motivated by guilt and might even last longer in missions. .

What does redemption mean? What picture does it convey? Often our first mistake is interpreting this word in light of our own culture or context. In the 21st century, what types of things do we redeem?

The first answer in our culture is coupons! We redeem slips of paper for a discounted price on our purchases. The second connotation is usually about redeeming mistakes or really bad situations.

If we take either of these definitions of redemption and plug them into our salvation, the result is cheapened. Do we really want to define our salvation as a coupon? And while in many ways, salvation does redeem a bad situation—Prior to knowledge of Christ, we were headed to hell—both of these modern cultural interpretations do not convey the depth of what redemption would mean to a member of the Roman church. As he was penning this letter, Paul did not sit around thinking about inventing a new Christian word. In fact, he did not invent the word redemption at all. It carried a meaning the first-century readers would clearly understand.

So what did it mean to the Roman believers?

In the first-century, the context of the word redemption came from the world of slavery. However, this was not the brutal picture of slavery that many of us have in our minds involving beatings and chains. First-century slavery was a normal part of life. They were more like paid servants, and it was a common way for those who needed to make money to provide for one's family. A slave would enter into an agreement with someone to serve for a set period of time, usually six years. Breaking this agreement through rebellion, theft, or running away carried severe penalties, even death. In spite of this, a slave could make a comfortable living in the first-century. To put it in modern terms, this was your first-century, blue-collar job.

However, the major difference from a normal job is the slave was not free. A slave entered into this contract at a slave market, where he or she would be auctioned to the highest bidder. It was a humiliating environment. The slave was stripped naked so the prospective owners could see his or her physical condition. While not as brutal as we usually picture it, it was not a pleasant place to spend the day.

The highest bidder won the right to enter into an agreement with the future servant, and after the agreement was made, the individual was no longer free to do whatever he or she wanted. The slave was bound by contract to serve his or her master. Failure to do so resulted in the swift and severe penalties previously mentioned.

Each slave owner possessed the right of redemption. If the owner wanted, he or she could purchase a redemption ticket with, "For Freedom," written on it. The master could inform the slave that he exercised the right of redemption. The master would give the ticket to their slave. He or she had already paid the money to employ the slave but chose to redeem him or her.

Another way to say this is that he paid a ransom for the slave[6]. The ransom bought the slave's freedom. When redemption was exercised, the slave could walk out of the slave market as a free man, never serving the master again.

You might ask, "What benefit is this to a slave seeking to provide for his family?"

The surprising thing about redemption is that the slave would still receive the wages and housing expressed in the contract, but he or she wouldn't have to do any of the work! History tells us this was a rare gift and honor, and after slaves were redeemed they would often go and live with their masters anyway. As they lived in the master's house, they would inevitably end up serving, sometimes doing the very same tasks which they were bought to do.

However, something changed within the heart of the servant. Redeemed slaves served from a place of freedom, not obligation or fear of punishment. No longer did they fear punishment. Rather, they freely served out of love for their masters. As John Piper says, "Gratitude is the correct response to the work of God, but we can never repay or should never even attempt to. We live right out of gratitude alone[7]."

History also tells us when a slave master died, a redeemed slave in the master's household received equal parts inheritance as a natural born son or daughter. They had been adopted into the master's family. Redemption was not merely an unexpected gift; it was life changing.

Was a slave required to live with the master? No. Redemption allowed her or she to walk out of the slave market and never see the master again. There were no obligations to the gift. It was free, and so was the slave.

This sounds much better than a coupon! There is nothing cheap in the meaning of the word redemption. As Paul chose to describe the salvation of the Jew and Gentile in Romans 3:23-24, "for all have sinned and fall short of the glory of God, and are justified by his grace as a gift, through the redemption that is in Christ Jesus." As they heard the word redemption, there was an immediate mental picture of a slave being bought out of slavery to be set free.

SET FREE FROM SIN

How does he use this metaphor to describe their salvation? Since their salvation is the same as ours, we can say this describes our salvation as well. We were all in the slave market of sin facing a life of slavery. We were doomed to a life of trying to pay off our sin through good works and deeds knowing this would never bring true freedom. Unless we were perfect slaves (which we have seen is impossible through animal crackers), we could expect punishment and ultimately death. Very quickly we would realize we need help. It doesn't take a rocket scientist to see the futile place we find ourselves in. In this place of desperation we cry out for redemption.

Into this slave market walks Jesus. He bids on us, using the most precious commodity at his disposal: his blood, his very life. With this as payment, he is undoubtedly a higher bidder than any other. He buys us. You could say he ransoms us. If the story ended at this point, we would be slaves to Christ.

Of course, the story does not stop there. Christ exercises, the right of redemption. Jesus hands us the ticket marked with the words. "For freedom." As 1 Peter 1:18-19 tells us, "Knowing that you were ransomed from the futile ways inherited from your forefathers, not with perishable things such as silver or gold, but with the precious blood of Christ, like that of a lamb without blemish or spot."

At this point, we have a choice to make. We are free. We have the gift of redemption. As a free person, we can walk out of the slave market and never see Christ again. Remember, there are no strings attached, nor any obligations. If we are free, we have to acknowledge it is possible to walk away and never serve the master.

However, knowing the value of the gift of redemption, the rarity and honor of this gift, why would we want to walk away? Rather, wouldn't we want to go and live with the master to serve Him? As we do, we might find ourselves doing some of the very things we would do if we were slaves, but something would have changed. It would not be the same as living as a slave. What is the difference?

Our motivation has changed. No longer would we serve because we must. We are not under a contract. We wouldn't feel a sense of obligation like a slave would. Now we serve because we want to. Our motivation would be love and gratitude, not fear or obligation. As Titus 2:14 says, "(He) who gave himself for us to redeem us from all lawlessness and to purify for himself a people for his own possession who are zealous for good works." We should want to obey, to do good works. Later in this book, we will explore the types of things we do to serve the master, but now let's stay focused on the motivation.

Our motivation would be love and gratitude, not fear or obligation.

It doesn't stop here. Just like a redeemed slave, we receive equal portions of the inheritance that God has for His children. There are no stepchildren in God's family. We are all legitimate sons and daughters (Ephesians 1:5). This too is reminiscent of adoption. We have been adopted into God's family, receiving everything He has to offer.

Personally, I have begun to understand my adoption by God in a deeper way after adopting my second son, Thabo. There is nothing in me that loves my biological son, Garett, anymore than Thabo. He has everything that I have to offer as a father. There are no second class sons in my family, nor are there in God's

Redemption is a jaw dropping, amazement inducing gift. Paul wants the Roman believers to take their eyes off the things that divide. A Roman church walking in gratitude will be less judgmental and critical of its fellow believers.

SO WHAT DO I NEED TO DO?

What did we do to receive this gift? What is our part? The answer is simple. We got saved. No earning, no working, and no striving. Redemption happens at salvation. That was the moment we were rescued out of the slave market of sin.

If you are reading these pages and you are a believer, you can have confidence that Jesus has redeemed you from the slave market. Colossians 1:14 echoes this thought, saying we believe in Christ "in whom we have redemption, the forgiveness of sins."

Redmption does require a response. Our objections that this is too easy need to be looked at; our motivations for our good deeds need to be evaluated. Receiving the gift of redemption does not guarantee a perfect life.

In Exodus 15:13, Moses says the Lord redeemed the people of Israel. They were bought with a price, ransomed out of Egypt brought through the Red Sea. God set them free to send them into the wilderness to meet with Him and eventually give them the land of Israel. Unfortunately, the response of the people quickly turned to complaining and sin. We see in the actions of the Israelites that they were far from perfect. I know some believers that would relate to this!

In 1 Corinthians 7:23, Paul uses the same imagery when challenging the believers to change their lifestyle. "You were bought with a price, do not become slaves of men." The implication is that redemption is final: do not go back to slavery!

Freedom does not guarantee that we will make the correct choice. But it does not put limits on the freedom. Israel did choose poorly. But they were not magically transported back to Egypt under Pharaoh for their sin. They still were free.

So for modern believers, what does this teach us? We need to change our motivations. We need to ask ourselves some of the following questions:

Why do we practice the disciplines of the Christian life?

Do we read our Bible because we fear punishment?

Do we pray to keep God happy so He will answer the requests we send him?

Do we find ourselves going to church or giving out of guilt?

None of these activities are wrong or sinful, but they can be done for the wrong reasons. As we continue looking at the passage in Romans, we will explore this further. Until then, I want to leave us with one question.

SON OR SLAVE?

If you were forced to describe your relationship with God using one of the two words below, which one would you pick?

A. Obligation
B. Freedom

Don't gloss over this question. Really ponder and consider your answer. Are you living in the place of a son or a slave? Do you practice the disciplines of the Christian life because you have to? Or can you say you want to, that you are compelled by love to do these things?

◉ ◉ ◉

Freedom does not guarantee that we will make the correct choice.

In summary, listen to the words of Jerry Bridges in his book *Transforming Grace*[8] when he says, "Only when we are convinced that the Christian life is lived by grace are we free to serve Him out of a loving and grateful heart."

The gift must be completely free. If it is not, we are bound by obligation to serve the master. This is not the picture redemption gives us. Believers were bought out of slavery with the purpose of setting them free. Freedom is the reason!

Live free. Live loved.

Questions for discussion

Do you ever feel like you're on a hamster wheel going nowhere in life? You know growth happens, but when are you going to reach your goal?

Think about the question posed at the end of the chapter. Which areas of your life do you live as a son and which are as a slave?

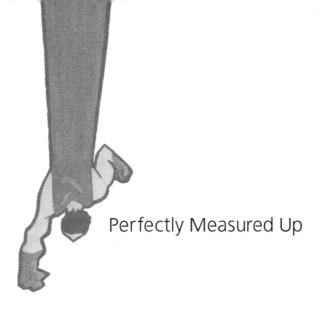

Perfectly Measured Up

Often, it seems our Christian lives become consumed by attempts to please God. Sunday school mantras of "read your Bible, pray every day, and you'll grow, grow, grow" echo through our minds.

How can we be confident God is pleased? In my travels and ministry, I meet very few people who express this confidence. Many avoid saying it for fear of sounding arrogant or self-centered.

The doctrine of justification tells us whether we are pleasing to God or not. Justification is a word that few believers hear regularly. Perhaps we have sung about it or heard it described as "just as if I never sinned." Unfortunately, true understanding seems rare. Many of us don't know how to understand this principle. If we attempt to impose a modern-day definition on justification, the importance is diminished. In a twenty-first century perspective, the following questions would be raised:

◎ ⊙ ◎

The legal definition of justification occurs when a judge finds someone innocent. He rises before all the witnesses of the court, making a public declaration that the one on trial is righteous, or innocent.

Is God justifying our bad decisions or wrong actions?

Do we try to make excuses for our stupidity?

Could this be the justification that Paul so loves in Romans?

These modern definitions seem too small for God. Let's look at a bit at Paul's thoughts.

Romans 3:23 says, "for all have sinned and fall short of the glory of God, and are justified by his grace as a gift, through the redemption that is in Christ Jesus."

Does God merely make excuses for our bad actions, saying, "Well, they are only human after all"?

Is it true that grace turns a blind eye to bad behavior?

That would be cheap grace. The truth of justification would have been culturally understood by the Jews and Gentiles that Paul is writing to in Romans. Just as redemption comes from the Greek world of slavery, justification also has a parallel in Greek society. This time, the word comes from the legal realm, the domain of the courts.

IN THE COURTROOM

In the Greek legal system, a trial is not decided by a jury of the people, but by a judge. The judge sits on the bench, obligated to obey the law and work with the facts. A good judge cannot be bought or swayed, and does not show favoritism. He must make his just decision based on the evidence. As the trial progresses, the evidence both for and against the accused is presented. Once the evidence is heard, the judge makes a decision. The legal definition of justification occurs when a judge finds someone innocent. He rises before all the witnesses of the court, declaring publicly that the one on trial is righteous, or innocent. This is the picture that gives us the meaning of justification. Paul chooses this word to describe the salvation of both Jews and Gentiles in his attempt to unify them, demonstrating that they have the same salvation. As they saw this word, their minds would immediately flash to the scene played out in the courtroom.

Let's use this picture to see what the great Apostle's teaching also means to us. In the spiritual sense, all of us found ourselves on trial before our salvation. God the judge presides on His throne. Being a good, law-abiding judge requires Him to look at the evidence and make His decision on the basis of the facts. Often salvation is looked upon as a pardon, as if God views us with pity. It is as if He says, "Oh all right, come on in." This would not be a just, evidence-based judge who makes his decision based on the facts. Instead a judge who plays favorites comes into view in this misrepresentation.

As God looks at us on trial, He examines the evidence of our lives that comes forth, both good and bad. As we know from the Old Testament, God's standard is perfection. Based on this, we should all receive a guilty verdict. We all sin and fall short. Sin is the same word as when we aim for the target, yet miss in archery[9]. We shoot for the target of perfection and miss the mark. We see this very clearly in our animal cracker illustration. We are not superheroes who are or will become perfect.

As we sit in the courtroom, we begin to sweat in expectation that the trial is not going to end favorably for us. Just as God the judge is about to make His decision, the verdict of guilty, we cry out in desperation.

"Help!"

"I need a savior! Will someone come to rescue me?"

From the back of the courtroom, the door bursts open. In walks Christ. He strides boldly to the front, comes up next to us, and beckons us to get out of our seat. We quickly obey. Sitting down in our place, Jesus substitutes himself for us. God, the judge on the bench, watches this change of events with interest, asking if there is any more evidence to be presented before He delivers His verdict. Now, with Christ in our place, it is no longer our evidence that is presented, but rather the evidence of Christ: his sinless life in action, word, thought, and attitude. After this evidence is presented, God the judge is ready to declare a verdict. He stands up in front of all the witnesses and speaks.

"Based on the evidence and facts presented, I make a public statement before all who are assembled that the one who is on trial is righteous, or innocent." Justification has just played out for us.

The gavel falls. The decision is final.

The trial is over; we have been declared innocent and forgiven. This is salvation! If you read this as a believer, this very scene has played out in heaven for you. God himself, based on Christ's evidence, has legally declared you justified.

What an incredible picture! God has made a public declaration of our justification. It is the same for all believers. Being saved means you are justified! By definition, this also implies that you have received righteousness! This is where we begin our spiritual journey.

F.F. Bruce says, "God pronounces believers righteous at the beginning of the course, not the end of it ... it cannot be on the basis of works they have not yet done ... such justification is purely an act of God's grace."

> It has nothing to do with their own personal holy lifestyle but the sinless life of Christ.

To the Roman Jews and Gentiles, they all have been equally justified. It has nothing to do with their own personal holy lifestyle but the sinless life of Christ. The unity in the equation comes through Christ. Neither Jews nor Gentiles posses a superior salvation.

Charles Spurgeon in his book All of Grace says, "We ... are always talking about our own goodness and our own worthiness, and we stubbornly hold to it that there must be something in us in order to win the notice of God. Now, God, who sees through all deceptions, knows that there is no goodness whatever in us ... He comes not because we are just, but to make us so."

Before we go too much further, we must get the full picture. Justification carries a public declaration of one's righteousness. To completely understand justification, we must also understand righteousness. Let's look at the meaning of this word next.

DO YOU MEASURE UP?

Righteousness reminds me of a story from my childhood. I grew up, like most children, with a love for amusement parks, especially the roller coasters. As I went to these parks with friends on warm summer days, it should have been the most carefree of times. Yet in the back of my mind, I had a concern. My friends would hurry through the park going from ride to ride. For me, as we approached each ride, there was a moment of hesitation. Most parks have certain cartoon character displays that serve a purpose for park goers who enter various rides. The park I went to had a chocolate theme. Those smiling candy bars would mock me at the entrance to each roller coaster. In their hand they held a scary sight: a ruler. My friends probably did not even know these characters existed. But as a vertically-challenged youngster, these rulers held my fate in their hands.

As I approached, I would do everything in my power to enhance my chances of success. I would begin walking on my tiptoes. I would mess up my afro-like hair in an attempt to get a little extra height. Whatever I thought would help me to measure up, I tried as I walked by the mocking candy bar.

And I made it.

Barely.

I was never denied, but it was close. Very close.

This story illustrates the way many of our Christian lives go. We do everything in our power to be acceptable to God. We hope and strive to try and measure up while deep down we wonder if we will be approved.

The beauty of righteousness answers the question of whether we measure up. We know we have been declared righteous in the courtroom. Now let's see how this helps us to meet the standard of God.

Righteousness has two separate definitions. One refers to God, and the other refers to man.

When God is called righteous, it means He is perfectly right in all He does. If God does it, it is right. End of discussion. This should not be too much of a theological stretch for us. God, who is good, only does right things. When we worship Him for his righteousness, we acknowledge this fact.

Righteousness when it refers to man is slightly different. It is defined as perfectly measuring up to a standard.

Imagine a ruler being held up to something, and we see it measures as perfectly straight. It meets the righteous standard. A plumb line in construction is used to keep walls vertical. It is a tool that shows if the wall meets the righteous standard of being vertical. A standard that is perfectly righteous makes the mark; no more, no less.

As Paul uses this term to define a believer's spiritual life, we see he says they perfectly measure up to God's standard. From our journey through the Old Testament, we know the standard of God is perfection. Righteousness sees believers as perfect! This includes every action, every thought, every word, and every attitude. If we fall short even in a single thought, we do not measure up. Perfect is perfect!

Remember God the judge is the one who has publicly declared this. If it were anyone else, it would be impossible. We see yet another picture of the forgiveness of God that is based on the work of Christ. Second Corinthians 5:21 tells us, "For our sake he made him to be sin who knew no sin, so that in him we might become the righteousness of God." The reason Christ took on our sin was so we could measure up to God's standard of perfection.

Sounds crazy! Bono, the lead singer of U2, put it well when he said, "Grace defies reason and logic." It does not make sense in our human mindset. Society teaches us nothing is free. Grace turns things upside down. Grace tells us that our attempts to be a superhero can die!

As I teach this in seminars, I love to ask the audience if they have ever looked at a crowd, and felt like someone was more spiritual than them. I think this is something many of us do. We feel better or worse when we compare ourselves to someone else. When viewing ourselves through the eyes of righteousness, it does not work. There is nothing we can do to be more (or less) measured up. Either we perfectly meet God's standard or we don't. Either you are saved or you are not.

> Grace turns things upside down. Grace tells us that our attempts to be a superhero can die!

Let's push it a bit. Is it difficult to imagine you wake up in the morning, look in the mirror, and call yourself righteous? Does that feel arrogant? There is no arrogance in that statement. It would be pride if righteousness comes on the basis on something we do or achieve.

What about being as righteous as our pastor? Are you cringing? The final straw may come when I ask you this.

Are you as righteous as Billy Graham? All over the world, the evangelist is held in such esteem that he may have already achieved sainthood! You may not have seen as many converts or spoken to stadiums full of people, but you are just as righteous. We are so trained that righteousness has something to do with us that we struggle with this understanding of grace.

There was a very popular worship song when I was growing up that is misunderstood. The first stanza says, "Holiness, holiness is what I long for. Holiness is what I need." Fine and good. Audiences or spontaneous gatherings will often embellish a bit in a second chorus. They change holiness to righteousness, singing it is what they long for or need. This leads to confusion.

Is this a worship song which declares they are not saved? I doubt it. When prompted by a worship leader to sing this refrain, I change the words privately to "righteousness is what I have." I believe this is a picture of true worship: truly giving thanks God for a gift that has nothing to do with me.

Tomorrow, practice preaching the gospel to yourself. Look in the mirror and proclaim that the handsome or beautiful face you see is righteous. It might feel strange, but it will be a reminder of the truth. Remember that if it were up to us, we would need to be men of steel. Good thing we are not expected to be superheroes.

QUESTIONS for discussion

Reflect back on the courtroom picture. Do we believe that God makes a legal decision for our lives based on the works of Christ? Or are we still judged on our own efforts? Talk about how it is difficult to accept someone else's acts of holiness (Christ's). What things or beliefs in our society make this even more difficult?

Do you struggle to see yourself as righteous? In what ways have you confused the idea of righteousness with things that you are responsible for? (if you struggle with this, the chapters to come deal with holiness, which might help).

⊙ ⊙ ⊙

"None but God would ever have thought of justifying me. I am a wonder to myself. I doubt not that grace is equally seen in others. Look at Saul of Tarsus, who foamed at the mouth, against God's servants. Like a hungry wolf, he worried the lambs and the sheep right and left, and yet God struck him down on the road to Damascus, changed his heart, and lived. He must often have marveled that he was justified by faith in Christ Jesus, for he was once a determined stickler for salvation by the works of the law. None but God would have ever thought of justifying such a man as Saul the persecutor; but the Lord God is glorious in grace."

CHARLES SPURGEON FROM *ALL OF GRACE*

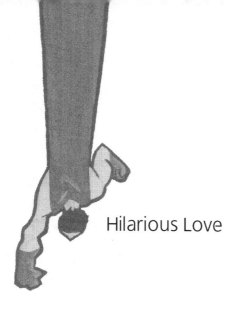

Hilarious Love

A smile appears on my face every time I remember a home video of my oldest son, Garett. He was about six months old, able to sit up on his own. I had these small balls that I put in my mouth and blew them in his direction. This was the funniest thing he had ever seen in his short existence. The belly laugh that came out of his little body was unbelievable. Of course, as a dad addicted to his laughing, I kept doing it. The funniest moment came when he toppled over in hysterics. The ball which shot out of my mouth was so hilarious he could not even remain sitting.

This picture reminds me of God. While not out of control, His love for us is so great that he can't even sit up. How does that thought sound to you? Sacrilegious? Blasphemous?

Or amazing! Let's dive back into Romans 3.

The final word we need to define in our study is propitiation. It is found in verse 25: "whom God put forward as a propitiation by his blood, to be received by faith."

What is propitiation?

We rush past this verse without any clue as to what it means. The New Revised Standard Version translates propitiation as sacrifice of atonement. It states that "Jesus was put forward as the sacrifice of atonement." I prefer this translation and will use it to explain the passage.

The sacrifice of atonement has two parts, the first being propitiation. It literally means "wrath taker." We could say Jesus is the one who takes away the wrath of God.

The second part deals with the change in God's emotions once wrath is gone. God is not emotionally neutral up in heaven. We know His anger is satisfied since His wrath is gone. But how does God feel?

Does He like us? Would He pick us to play on His sports team?

The word that is translated "atonement" or "propitiation" stems from he Greek word "hilasterion".[10] This word relates to the Old Testament image of the mercy seat and can also be related to reconciliation. Jesus shows us mercy through being our sacrifice of atonement, which restores the relationship broken by sin between God and man.

The Christians from the church in Rome would be familiar with this idea from both the Old Testament and first-century culture. Culturally, the idea originates with Greek mythology. In these legends, hilasterion relates to the emotions of the gods changing from negative to a state of hilarious happiness. In mythology, the gods would need to be manipulated for this to occur. Their emotions would never change as a free act of grace. This would cost the people greatly.

Paul uses the word hilasterion to illustrate God's emotions being changed towards believers. Some define hilasterion as an overwhelming, over flowing, out-of-control love. God is no longer angry, with the need to execute wrath. Christ has taken that wrath on himself. When He did this, God's emotions towards believers changed to a nearly indescribable love. Our best attempt leads us to the word hilasterion. God is so pleased and so in love with us that the English equivalent would say, 'God is hilarious with love over us.' The English word "hilarious" has its roots in this Greek word hilasterion.

> God is no longer angry, with the need to execute wrath. Christ has taken that wrath on himself.

Remember the image of my son, unable to contain his laughter? He could not stay upright because the ball flying out of my mouth towards him was so hilarious. This is the mental picture I have of God with hilasterion love. It does not remove my reverence and awe for the Creator of the universe. It adds to it the reality of the sacrifice of atonement; God the Father hilarious with love over all believers.

Common sense tells us to climb; grace tells us we can get off the ladder.

I often meet believers who feel like God is out to get them, people who subconsciously wait for the lightning bolt from heaven to strike them down over past sin. Many times, we view God's love for us as tolerance. We picture our heavenly Father as an annoyed parent who puts up with youngsters who misbehave.

These views of God often come from our limited perspective and earthly examples. God is not like our earthly fathers.

When Christ satisfied the wrath of God, it was completely gone. In its place came hilasterion, an overwhelming, over flowing, and out-of-control love.

Is this too good to be true?

How can this happen for free?

We think God will only be pleased with us if we deserve it. We believe we need to climb the ladder and be good Christians, earning his favor.

Wrong.

Salvation comes as a free gift. We need to receive it! If this were anyone else's idea it would be too good to be true.

Common sense tells us to climb; grace tells us we can get off the ladder. The gospel truly is good news. Sin remains the largest of problems, but the solution is more than up to the task.

BACK TO ROMANS

Now that we have defined our terms and understand them in their historical context, let's put the pieces of our puzzle together. Return to our main passage in Romans 3 so can see the complete thought Paul was trying to communicate. As we read through the passage again, you will see I have done something different. Instead of the "big" words, I have substituted the definitions. Read it slowly and allow the truth of what Paul wanted to show the Romans believers to sink in.

> But now measuring up to the standard of God has been made real apart from the law, although the Law and the Prophets bear witness to it, perfectly measuring up to the standard of God through faith in Jesus Christ for all who believe. For there is no distinction: for all have sinned and fall short of the glory of God, and are declared publicly by the judge to have perfectly measured up to God's standard by undeserved kindness as a gift, through the buying out of slavery in order to be set free in Christ Jesus, whom God put forward as the one who took away the wrath of God and

replaced it with an overflowing, overwhelming, out-of-control love by his blood, to be received by faith. This was to show that God is right in everything He does, because in his divine knowledge he had passed over former sins. It was to show that God is right in everything He does at the present time, so that he might publicly declare that one who has faith in Jesus has perfectly measured up to God's standard. (Romans 3:21-26 paraphrased)

Wow!

We may have just read the most power-packed few sentences in all of scripture.

Jerry Bridges speaks of our need for repetition and reminders when he urges believers to "preach the gospel to themselves every day."[11] This is a "speak the truth to yourself" kind of message.

We need to know and remember the truth, which brings defeat to the lies of the enemy. We will not succumb to Satan's tactics if we remind ourselves of our identity in Christ. When we preach the gospel to ourselves, it is spiritual warfare.

Paul himself does this in the book of Ephesians. If there were ever a city in need of spiritual warfare, it would have been Ephesus. It was the pagan worship capital of the first century. Believers struggled with how to live successful

Christian lives. Paul responds to these issues, as he spends the first three chapters of Ephesians to remind them what to believe. Eventually he gets to prayer, lifestyle, and the armor of God. These are all very important parts of a believer's life. Yet the portion of time he spends to refresh the Ephesians on the gospel of salvation shows how important it is in their daily lives. If they know and walk in truth, they will be less likely to fall captive to the lies of the enemy!

I would like to go over Romans 3 one more time. Let's preach the gospel to ourselves again. This time, I will format the text a bit differently. I urge you to read through this part slowly and meditatively. Let these truths sink in deeply to your heart and mind.

> But now the righteousness (perfectly measuring up to the standard) of God, has been made real apart from the law (not by the sacrifice of animal crackers. We tried and it did not work!), although the Law and the Prophets bear witness to it (the entire Old Testament pointed towards the reality of Christ) the righteousness (perfectly measuring up to the standard) of God through faith in Jesus Christ for all who believe. For there is no distinction (there is no one more or less righteous): For all have sinned and fall short of the glory of God (we all began in the same place of sin), and are justified (declared publicly to have perfectly

measured up to God's standard in the courtroom)
by his grace (undeserved kindness and unmerited,
unearned favor) as a gift, through the redemption
(being bought out slavery in order to be set free)
that is in Christ Jesus, whom God put forward as
sacrifice of atonement (the one who took away
the wrath of God and replaced it with an overflowing, overwhelming, out-of control-love) by
his blood, to be received by faith. This was to
show that God is righteous (right in everything
He does), because in his divine knowledge he had
passed over former sins (He wanted to forgive
sin). It was to show that God is righteous (right in
everything He does) at the present time, so that
He might justify (publicly declare) that the one
who has faith in Jesus has perfectly measured
up to God's standard (his standard of perfection
in every action done, every word spoken, every
thought, every attitude and emotion of heart,
and even against the sin that comes from Adam.
He is perfectly measured up.). (Romans 3:21-26
paraphrased)

Wow.

Take a deep breath. Sigh a good sigh. The gospel is not
merely good news, it is great news.

Do we believe God's truth rather than the standards and
requirements given to us by society?

Which filter do we look through when we look at God, other people, and even ourselves? Is it the filter of truth or experience?

If it is not the filter of scripture, we must change and begin to think as God thinks. Nowhere in this statement of salvation from Paul do we find anything of our own effort from which we can take credit. There is no place for pride. We are not superheroes.

Unmerited favor and undeserved kindness: this is the definition of grace.

Listen to the words of F.F. Bruce as we ponder the depths of grace: "When it comes to the question of our acceptance by God, how much more satisfying it is to know oneself justified freely by his grace than to hope to be ... in the later case, I can never be really satisfied, that my behavior has been sufficiently meritorious as to win divine approval ... Even if I do the best I can, how can I be certain ... I may hope, but can never be sure. But if in God's grace he assures me of his acceptance in advance, and I embrace it, then I can go on to do his will without worrying if I am adequate enough."

What's the big deal?

Why is this so important?

Listen to these quotes from Neil Anderson in his book *Breaking the Bondage of Legalism*. These are from various interviews with Christian college students. Look at these shocking statistics.[12]

55% of people believe salvation must be earned.

> Nowhere in this statement of salvation from Paul do we find anything of our own effort from which we can take credit.

60% of Christian college students feel guilty for sins they committed in the past always, often, or sometimes.

58% of Christians said they feel they do not measure up to God's standard.

This is not merely a discipleship issue. These things go to the very core of a believer's faith. Essentially, these students doubt the saving work of Christ in their lives. They, like society, believe nothing is for free. These statistics show they believe there must be something they can do to improve on the work of Christ.

THE ARMOR OF GOD

Before we wrap up this chapter, let's take a quick look back at Ephesians. I mentioned how Paul went to great lengths to remind the Ephesians of truth as a weapon in spiritual warfare. Then, in Ephesians 6, he finishes his encouragement with the passage known as the armor of God. Today, we tend to miss that this was a summary of what was already said. In churches, we are exhorted as believers to "put on the armor every day." I have heard people exclaim, "I've got my armor on," as a badge of merit.

> Therefore take up the whole armor of God, that you may be able to withstand in the evil day, and having done all, to stand firm. Stand therefore, having fastened on the belt of truth, and having put on the breastplate of righteousness, and, as shoes for your feet, having put on the readiness given by the gospel of peace. In all circumstances take up the shield of faith, with which you can extinguish all the flaming darts of the evil one; and take the helmet of salvation, and the sword of the Spirit, which is the word of God. (Ephesians 6:13-17)

Notice what all the pieces are described as. The pieces are about truth, righteousness, the gospel, faith, salvation, and the Word of God. This is not about what we do!

When we consider this, one might wonder: when we put on the armor, do we ever take it off?

Of course not. You and I do not remove our salvation when we lie down to sleep at night. This truth brings a reminder of what we already have in Christ.

2 Peter 1:3 tells us, "His divine power has granted to us all things that pertain to life and godliness, through the knowledge of him who called us to his own glory and excellence."

Wearing the armor does not constitute a work, but is rather a celebration of the work of Christ. We don't take it off. We have everything we need for success. May God give us all a deeper revelation grace which tells us we have perfectly measured up to His standard.

QUESTIONS for discussion

Does our limited perspective on love make it difficult to fully grasp the change in God's emotions from wrath to a hilarious love for us?

Reread the paraphrase of Romans 3, the one with all the editorial statements. What is your honest response to these words? Do you believe them or are they too good to be true?

Is it Really That Big?

In Victor Hugo's classic novel, *Les Miserables*, the criminal Jean Valjean is released from prison and wanders the streets looking for a place to stay. No one will take in a former convict, though his only crime was hunger, having stolen bread to eat. Eventually, a kind priest houses him. When the priest has gone to sleep, Jean Valjean takes his silver and flees the priest's home. Valjean is later captured with the stolen silver and brought back to the priest by the police. When the priest realizes what is happening, he has a curious response.

"So there you are! I'm delighted to see you. I see you have the silverware, but had you forgotten that I gave you the candlesticks as well? They are silver like the rest. Did you forget them?"

Once the police leave, the priest gives him the candle-sticks and urges him to use the money to make himself an honest man. Jean Valjean's life is radically transformed by the power of grace. A former convict turns into a purveyor of grace.[13] The entire story carries a grand illustration of law versus grace. Grace has the power to change the past and even the future.

We all know and agree that at the moment of salvation, our past sins are forgiven. The slate is wiped clean and we start fresh.

What of future sin? What of sin we have not committed yet? Is this covered or is there another formula we need to know?

Paul, in his letter to the Romans, anticipates some of these questions will come. He knows as he enlarges people's perspective on grace, it turns their worldview upside down. He then turns his attention to Abraham in chapter 4 as a case study.

WHAT ABOUT FUTURE SIN?

Paul uses Abraham as an example because the Jewish half of his audience reveres him as the ultimate Jew. The other half can easily see Abraham was saved by faith not works. Look at Romans 4:1-3.

"What then shall we say was gained by Abraham, our forefather according to the flesh? For if Abraham was justified by works, he has something to boast about, but not before God. For what does the Scripture say? Abraham believed God, and it was counted to him as righteousness."

The word we want to focus on is "counted" in verse 3. Other versions use terms such as reckoned and credited. This word comes from the accounting world in the first century. If you visit an accountant, he would pull out your ledger sheet, and you could see all your debts and your payments. In making payment for all your debts, this would bring the total owed to zero. This declares the account balanced or reconciled. We still do not have an account that has been reckoned.

Imagine you write a check for a bill where you owe $10. Somehow, you misread the bill and make the check for $100. The $10 that was owed is paid in full, but $90 remains left over. Does that extra amount become a tip for the accountant?

That extra $90 will appear in your account as a credit balance. The next time you buy something, it will automatically be paid for out of the credit balance. This $90 is real money you can use in your account.

This picture gives us our definition of the word reckoned, or credited. The account is overpaid, with a credit balance that remains and can be used. Paul uses this first-century word to describe what occurred at Abraham's conversion. All of his past sins were forgiven. This would bring the account in balance. Paul takes it a step further as he shows his account more than balanced, it was credited with righteousness at salvation. This credit is bigger than the account being balanced!

We already know that righteousness means perfectly measuring up to God's standard of perfection. Imagine the scene in heaven at Abraham's salvation. The accounting books are opened, and past sin is erased. Real righteousness is placed in his account. At that moment, Abraham is sinless, but this is not the end of the story.

Abraham lived as a normal man today. He continued to sin after salvation. When he commits additional sins, God turns to his page in the book, about to write the sin down.

He stops! What does He see?

He sees righteousness, which is perfect conformity to a standard. The account has been reckoned; sin is already taken care of. This is based on real righteousness being in his account. There is no need to write down sin that has already been forgiven.

Is this too good to be true? Is there a chance someone would try to abuse this amazing grace?

Before we argue too loudly, let's look a deeper into Abraham's life. If being reckoned is true, we should be able to see it in the pages of Scripture.

ABRAHAM

Let's turn to Genesis 15:1-6 to see how this plays out.

> After these things the word of the Lord came to Abram in a vision: Fear not, Abram, I am your shield; your reward shall be very great. But Abram said, O Lord God, what will you give me, for I continue childless, and the heir of my house is Eliezer of Damascus? And Abram said, Behold, you have given me no offspring, and a member of my household will be my heir. And behold, the word of the Lord came to him: This man shall not be your heir; your very own son shall be your heir. And he brought him outside and said, Look toward heaven, and number the stars, if you are

> able to number them. Then he said to him, So
> shall your offspring be. And he believed the Lord,
> and he counted it to him as righteousness.

These verses quoted in Romans 4 contain the story of Abraham's salvation. We don't see Jesus mentioned, but let's look closer. What do we see?

God gives Abraham a promise of descendants as numerous as the stars. He puts his faith in this promise. God then counts his faith as meeting the qualification for salvation. The gift of righteousness is included in this new found salvation. In actuality, Abraham put his faith in Christ without knowing all the details. We will see this as we move ahead in Abraham's life. First, let's put ourselves into Abraham's sandals.

Imagine you are Abraham, having just experienced this amazing salvation. If this were a movie, the music in the background would reach its crescendo. Abraham would raise his hands towards heaven in worship! Can you see it? As the music dies down, what does Abraham as a newly-saved follower of God do in response to the promise of descendants?

Let's not get too spiritual now. I imagine he said something like this: "Hey Sarah, wait until you hear what God just said! Let's go have a romantic dinner in the tent, and afterwards I will tell you all about it!" They got together and tried to make some babies! Even in the Old Testament, the birds and the bees worked the same way.

Fast forward now to chapter 16:1-4 of Genesis:

"Now Sarai, Abram's wife, had borne him no children. She had a female Egyptian servant whose name was Hagar. And Sarai said to Abram, Behold now, the Lord has prevented me from bearing children. Go in to my servant; it may be that I shall obtain children by her. And Abram listened to the voice of Sarai. So, after Abram had lived ten years in the land of Canaan, Sarai, Abram's wife, took Hagar the Egyptian, her servant, and gave her to Abram her husband as a wife. And he went in to Hagar, and she conceived."

Did you notice the length of time mentioned in this passage? "After Abram had lived ten years in the land ... " Chapter 15 of Genesis shows us a glorious salvation experience and promise for countless descendants. It also leaves Abraham excited to do his part in creating ancestors. Chapter 16 begins ten years later, with no children. Ten years is a long time to try to have children without success.

Sarah conceives an idea, and Abraham listens to her (Genesis 16:1-4). She suggests he have children with another woman, her slave Hagar. Abraham heeds the counsel of Sarah and has a son named Ishmael.

We have a saved and righteous Abraham making some mistakes here. He sins multiple times. His first mistake occurs when he listens to Sarah over God. He tries to help

God fulfill His promises in a way which was never intended. Abraham commits adultery by having sex with a woman who is not his wife. This is mistake number two. In this culture, it was a common occurrence, but this practice did not line up with God's standards. In the Garden of Eden, God sanctioned marriage to be exclusive between one man and one woman. Abraham broke this standard.

Abraham is not a perfect man after salvation. He sins. The chapter concludes by telling us Ishmael was born when Abraham was 86 years old (verse 16).

Chapter 17 picks up the story when Abraham is 99 years old. Thirteen more years have passed. We are looking at a minimum of 23 years of hoping God would fulfill His promise. Twenty-three years and still no son. I am sure we can imagine the frustration on Abraham's part. Here is what we can see in chapter 17:15-19:

> And God said to Abraham, As for Sarai your wife, you shall not call her name Sarai, but Sarah shall be her name. I will bless her, and moreover, I will give you a son by her. I will bless her, and she shall become nations; kings of peoples shall come from her. Then Abraham fell on his face and laughed and said to himself, Shall a child be born to a man who is a hundred years old? Shall Sarah, who is ninety years old, bear a child? And Abraham said to God, Oh that Ishmael might live before you!

God said, No, but Sarah your wife shall bear you a son, and you shall call his name Isaac. I will establish my covenant with him as an everlasting covenant for his offspring after him.

When Abraham is 99 years old, God comes and repeats his promise. Abraham's response this time is a bit different. He falls on his face and laughs! He reminds God of his age and the condition of his body as he begs him to accept Ishmael as the chosen one.

God says "No."

He will fulfill the promise as He stated 23 years earlier. This promise is a part of something much bigger. The son will "give rise to nations, kings of people will come from him," and "he will usher in an everlasting covenant." Abraham did not see Jesus as we know Him in his salvation experience, but today, we see how his faith in this promise eventually led to the Messiah.

Something to note here is the consequences of Abraham's sin in spite of God's forgiveness. God forgives Abraham for adultery, but the consequences of that sin are real. Ishmael is alive and well. God, in an amazing statement of forgiveness and grace, blesses Ishmael. As we continue our journey in Genesis, we see Abraham's eventual son of the promise, Isaac, and Ishmael will not get along. They will become the worst of enemies. The consequences of sin have impact in time and space, so much so we still see the effect today. Today's Jews descend from Isaac and today's Arabs from Ishmael. They are still fighting.

Sin has consequences. Forgiveness is not a "get out of jail free" card. Abraham's sin has had over 4,000 years worth of consequences.

Wait a second

We've journeyed with Abraham through several life events in Genesis. Now, let's return to Romans to observe how Paul is going to use Abraham being reckoned as righteous to make his point. We pick it up back in Romans 4:18-21 as Paul describes Abraham:

"In hope he believed against hope, that he should become the father of many nations, as he had been told, So shall your offspring be. He did not weaken in faith when he considered his own body, which was as good as dead (since he was about a hundred years old), or when he considered the barrenness of Sarah's womb. No distrust making him waver concerning the promise of God, but he grew strong in his faith as he gave glory to God, fully convinced that God was able to do what he had promised."

Did you notice anything of interest in this passage? Read it again. Is this the same Abraham we just read about in Genesis?

Paul describes him as "believing against hope, not weakening in faith, no distrust made him waver and being fully convinced."

Look closely at the "not weakening in faith" part. It tells us which moment of Abraham's story was being referred to. Paul says he "did not weaken when considering his own body which was dead because he was 90." We know the exact event this was in reference to.

Except he did weaken. Genesis says Abraham fell on his face and laughed. Wait a second! Is this an error in Scripture?

Surely Paul must have forgotten what happened in Genesis. But Paul was a Pharisee before his conversion, and he would have had the entire first five books of Moses memorized by the age of twelve. Paul didn't forget.

Perhaps Paul really liked Abraham. Maybe he was the president of the Abraham fan club. His tent may have been plastered with posters of Abraham. Maybe he only wanted to remember the good things Abraham did, forgetting the bad.

How could Paul, under the inspiration of the Holy Spirit, say these things?

Perhaps this is his point.

Let's remember why Paul is using Abraham as an example. He was made righteous by his faith, not works. Righteousness means all his past and future sins are

DEATH OF THE MODERN SUPERHERO

forgiven. Paul views Abraham through the perspective of God! Righteousness is so real it is as if Abraham never fell on his face and laughed. We've already established sin has consequences, but here we see the other side of God as he deals with sin. Sin is forgiven and forgotten. Consequences of sin are horizontal and affect things here on earth. In the vertical, between us and God, righteousness is so real that Paul can say Abraham "believed against hope, did not weaken in faith, no distrust made him waver and he was fully convinced."

Righteousness is so real it is as if Abraham never fell on his face and laughed.

We struggle to forgive and forget in our relationships, but God does not. If salvation does not cover future sin, we have a problem. To follow the illustration of this book, we would need to go back to sacrifice animal crackers! That did not work for salvation. Why would it work to keep our salvation?

It reminds me of an illustration Rob Bell uses in his book *Velvet Elvis*. He gives the scenario of being at a restaurant, enjoying a meal. The waiter approaches and tells you someone has paid your bill. You have a choice to make. You can receive the gift with gratitude and trust that it is done, or you can choose to not believe it. It seems absurd to consider lodging a protest in unbelief. Yet, in our Christian walks, the same scenario happens. The bill is paid. We are forgiven. Often we continue in our attempts to pay the bill through our good works or obedience. It sounds arrogant to assume we could somehow improve the work of Christ. Instead, we must trust the work is done. We can rest in this reality that the debt is gone. This is what being reckoned as righteous is all about. We don't need to be a superhero, but we do need to receive the gift!

But don't we need to repent?

Must we confess our sins and repent so we will be forgiven?

Confession and acknowledgement of our sin is an essential part of a believer's conversion. Once we are saved, is confession of every sin required to continue in that forgiveness?

Let's think about the animal cracker illustration. Every action, thought, word, and attitude required a sacrifice. If repentance is required, then the same standard of perfection holds true. We must specifically repent of each sinful action, word, thought, and attitude. Missing even one would break God's standard. For us to utter a prayer such as, "God, forgive me for all my sins"; just won't cut it.

Let's give some flesh to this idea. Imagine if every night I pray and ask God to forgive me for all my sins, and try to name them to the best of my ability. I go to sleep each night forgiven. The next day, I wake up, go to school, and in the course of the day, sin. On my way home, a bus runs me over, and I die. I have not confessed my sin for the day. Do I go to hell? If repentance is a requirement, the answer would be yes. But that sounds absurd.

Listen to the words of Charles Spurgeon: "Repentance will not make you see Christ; but to see Christ will give you repentance. You may not make a Christ out of your repentance, but you must look to Christ for repentance."

Repentance is a healthy response when God convicts us of sin...

A requirement for forgiveness? No.

Grace is bigger than our attempts to confess sin. Repentance is a healthy response when God convicts us of sin, one that shows our desire to change and be more like Him.

This does not give us an excuse to sin or do away with obedience. Our obedience never earned us the love of God, it has always been our response to a love that we already have. God still desires us to make holiness our goal. It is the vision or target we set before us. In our Christian lives, we should move closer to this goal. We cannot forget that a goal is different from a requirement. Jesus himself told us, "You therefore must be perfect, as your heavenly Father is perfect" (Matthew 5:48). Jesus made us perfect when he declared us righteous through justification. While never actually achieving perfection in our behavior on Earth, Jesus accomplishes what we are unable to do. Our response of gratitude focuses our eyes on this standard of Christ-likeness; its our goal to become more like him as we love and serve him.

The Unforgivable Sin

Have you ever found yourself in fear that you or someone you know has committed the unforgivable sin?

As we are promote a grace that is so huge and amazing, it is only a matter of time until someone will raise the question of the "unforgivable sin." Rightly so. If there is one act that can undo the amazing picture of grace we've explored, we must look into it.

Fear of committing the unpardonable goes a bit like this: In a moment of doubt or trial, you uttered a statement that has haunted you ever since. In the back of your mind, you are concerned that God will not forgive this indiscretion. If you identify with this feeling, you can empathize with many believers who walk in fear.

Will you face God someday and hear Him tell you to depart, for you did the unpardonable?

The passage in question comes from Mark 3:28-29: "Truly, I say to you, all sins will be forgiven the children of man, and whatever blasphemies they utter, but whoever blasphemes against the Holy Spirit never has forgiveness, but is guilty of an eternal sin."

What exactly was Jesus making reference to when He spoke this strange statement? Was he on a journey towards Jerusalem to face his impending death when suddenly he realized he had forgotten one indispensable teaching?

"Hey guys, I've got to let you know about the one thing you never want to do." He explains this and then says, "Ok, let's keep going."

This is probably not how it took place.

One essential principle used to bring understanding to difficult passages in the Bible is to consider the context. Context comes when you've read the verses before and after the passage. This gives us a better idea of what events were happening when the statements were made. Context is essential to good interpretation. Most cults and strange doctrines have been started based on Biblical passages with the wrong interpretation due to lack of consideration for context. So let us consider the context of this passage starting in Mark 3:20:

> Then he went home, and the crowd gathered again, so that they could not even eat. And when his family heard it, they went out to seize him, for they were saying, He is out of his mind. And the scribes who came down from Jerusalem were saying, He is possessed by Beelzebub, and by the

prince of demons he casts out the demons. And he called them to him and said to them in parables, How can Satan cast out Satan? If a kingdom is divided against itself, that kingdom cannot stand. And if a house is divided against itself, that house will not be able to stand. And if Satan has risen up against himself and is divided, he cannot stand, but is coming to an end. But no one can enter a strong man's house and plunder his goods, unless he first binds the strong man. Then indeed he may plunder his house. Truly, I say to you, all sins will be forgiven the children of man, and whatever blasphemies they utter, but whoever blasphemes against the Holy Spirit never has forgiveness, but is guilty of an eternal sin—for they had said, He has an unclean spirit. (Mark 3:20-30)

The event under consideration has the scribes saying Jesus was doing miracles by the power of Beelzebub, or Satan. Jesus responds to these accusations in a parable, as he illustrates that any team divided will fail. He concludes his defense with the statement about blasphemy. Now if we look at the verse immediately after the passage, it will help our interpretation. Verse 30 tells us why Jesus says what he does: "for they had said, He has an unclean spirit." They had just levied this accusation against him. The "they" was in reference to his family, who attempted to restrain him, as well as his accusers; the scribes. So we see this statement is not a random, unsolicited comment, but rather a direct response to the situation at hand.

Before we see how this applies to us today, let's take an even wider look at context. When we come upon unclear passages in Scripture, we always need to keep the big picture of Scripture in mind for our interpretations.

In the Bible, do we see other sins being called unforgivable? Does Scripture give a distinction on the levels of sin?

Romans 6:23 makes it very clear when it says, "for the wages of sin is death." There is no distinction. All sin is punishable by death. The pages of Scripture also promise forgiveness to anyone who asks.

How can we interpret the blasphemy passage?

Jesus spoke directly to people who accused him of doing his ministry by the power of Satan. He told them they could never be forgiven. We know from the rest of Scripture that if they repented, they would indeed be forgiven. The apostle Paul is the best example of this. If anyone blasphemed, it was Paul (then known as Saul). Rather than a statement directed towards a specific sin, Jesus dealt with a person's faith. Remember, the accusations were of him of being Satan. If someone believed Jesus to be Satan, it would be impossible to be forgiven. You would not believe Jesus is God and the source of all forgiveness. Not being forgiven would constitute an eternal sin. All sin not under the power of Christ can be considered an eternal sin; it is never forgiven and goes with you to the grave and judgement. To put it simply, in their current state of belief, these people would never find the forgiveness of sin.

If they no longer believe that Christ is Satan, can they find eternal life?

The two groups of people being addressed here are Jesus's family and scribes. We know from later in Scripture that James, the brother of Christ, wrote an epistle. Jesus's mother was at the cross and seemed to understand the full picture of who her son was. These people were indeed forgiven.

We also see in the gospels that a scribe was told he was close to the kingdom of God in Mark 12:28-34. If this blasphemy was truly an unforgivable sin, this could not have occurred. We would have to conclude that Jesus lied to the man!

Look how the other gospels support this interpretation. The writers record a summary in their accounts of what Jesus taught. "Whoever is not with me is against me, and whoever does not gather with me scatters" (Luke 11:23, Matthew 12:30).

This further illustrates the trend in scripture we discussed in chapter four. The pattern shows all of humanity exists in one of two groups. In this particular case, it becomes quite clear. One group has sins that are forgiven and the other, unforgiven.

So do you need to walk in fear in reference to the unforgivable sin?

If you know you are a believer in Christ, then the answer is a resounding no. To believe so would imply there is some sin that falls outside of the sacrifice of Christ. If this is the case, we must go back to making sacrifices for our sins.

Do you want to go back to animal crackers?

Whatever doubts cross your mind, past or present, they are already forgiven. Doubts and questions are a part of life; they are not a threat to God. I believe He delights in them. The presence of such questions indicates we are search of greater revelation and knowledge of the Lord. Questions are a part of the pursuit of God.

Rest easy.

Grace is big.

We don't have to be superheroes to keep it!

◉ QUESTIONS for discussion

Why do we find it difficult to believe that being reckoned as righteous covers our future sins as well as those in the past?

Confess the ways you are still trying to be a superhero.

Can I Do Whatever I Want?'

"Once Saved, Always Saved."

"He is a backslider."

"If they walk away from God, they were never really saved."

We hear these kinds of statements in an attempt to make sense of the mystery of God. This chapter dives into the age-old debate of once saved, always saved versus losing one's salvation. My goal is not to convert you to one view or the other, but to show how there can be peace and security in salvation. As we are explore the topic of grace, it is natural for questions on this topic to arise.

"How big is grace?"

"Is there a line you just cannot cross?"

"As believers, can we do whatever we want?"

Even in Scripture, Paul anticipates his churches would have these questions. He lays out his presentation of the gospel in all its glory in Romans. Yet in chapter 6, we see he anticipates the "can I do whatever I want" question.

"What shall we say then? Are we to continue in sin that grace may abound? By no means! How can we who died to sin still live in it?" (Romans 6:1-2).

Salvation is not a fragile thing you lose by accident.

The phrase translated "by no means" is a rather mild translation. The literal words carry a much harsher tone such as, "God forbid!"[14] God forbid that after we look into the depth of salvation and grace, our response would be to abuse it by doing whatever we want. Through this question, Paul tells people to return to school and learn the basics again.

Regardless of your opinion on this controversial topic, there are several basic principles we can all agree on. Salvation is not a fragile thing you lose by accident. We do not need to fear God's response on Judgment Day. We will explore passages in 1 Timothy and Hebrews to find truths we can all agree on.

Our search begins with two passages in 1 Timothy.

"By rejecting this, some have made shipwreck of their faith, among whom are Hymenaeus and Alexander, whom

I have handed over to Satan that they may learn not to blaspheme" (1 Timothy 1:19-20).

"Now the Spirit expressly says that in later times some will depart from the faith by devoting themselves to deceitful spirits and teachings of demons" (1 Timothy 4:1).

In both these passages, we can see a common theme. The issue being addressed is not an issue of sin but of faith. Both passages talk of some people who depart or shipwreck their faith. These are not the specific sins we see Paul dealing with other places in Scripture, but are rather issues of faith. As you search scripture for verses which seem pertinent to this debate, you will find they involve issues of faith, not sin. Sin can be forgiven; we know this clearly from our study of justification, righteousness, and being reckoned.

But if you change your faith, what does that mean?

The most common emotion associated with this debate is fear. I know many believers who lie awake at night in anxiety whether they will make it when the Lord returns. Even the term "losing your salvation" brings fear. If we lose something, it implies an accidental memory lapse or forget- fulness. I do not purposely lose my keys. If we can accidentally misplace something as valuable as our salvation, we would have good reason to fear!

Imagine you wake up one morning and shout, "Where is my salvation? I cannot find it anywhere!" This leads us to believe that questions, doubts, or times of trial can take us out of the kingdom of God. It would be easy to slip into a victim mentality if this were the case.

IMPOSSIBLE TO RESTORE?

The letter to the Hebrews also deals with this issue in chapter 6:4-6 where it speaks of the "impossibility of finding repentance." We will see the Hebrews did not struggle with an accidental losing but a cognitive change of faith.

"For it is impossible to restore again to repentance those who have once been enlightened, who have tasted the heavenly gift, and have shared in the Holy Spirit, and have tasted the goodness of the word of God and the powers of the age to come, if they then fall away, since they are crucifying once again the Son of God to their own harm and holding him up to contempt."

What is this impossibility the author refers to?

The Epistle to the Hebrews was written to a group of Christians who were being tempted to return to Judaism. When they received salvation, they left families, jobs, and culture. When you are Jewish, all of life is Jewish. It is not merely a thing you do on Sundays. History tells us that when Jews converted, their families would literally hold a funeral service for them. They were as good as dead. If they considered a return to Judaism, it would give these people their families, cultures, and jobs back.

The author says if they leave Christianity and go back to Judaism, it is impossible to find repentance. This would be true in any other religion or system. The only place forgiveness or repentance can be found is in Christ. To the first-century Christians, the message is clear. There are two groups of people: forgiven and unforgiven. You are forgiven in Christ. Stay there! This is why we see repeated warnings to endure and persevere in the epistle to the Hebrews. To leave Christianity meant you walked away from the only system in which you could find repentance or forgiveness. Stay where you are and have no fear. The Hebrews were not being tempted with a particular sin; they were facing the potential to change their faith.

The term that is used to indicate the possibility one could renounce their faith is apostasy. This word indicates a deliberate, calculated, continual walking away from God. You know what you are doing, and you keep doing it without looking back. The picture we see here is not of someone who wonders if they are still saved. The apostate does not care. Perhaps the most important word in this definition is continual. This is not a doubt, a time of fear, or a season of struggle. The picture shows one who has walked away and does not look back.

We do see a few examples of people who walked away for a season in scripture but came back. Peter denied he even knew Christ three times, but went on to write books of the Bible and became an early leader in the church. Jonah ran as far as he could in the world from God, yet returned to see one of the greatest single-day revivals in history in the city of Nineveh. These men turned their back on God, but did not do it continually. Grace was big enough to keep them in the kingdom.

"What of those who live in a sinful way and do not care?"

"Are you saying they are still saved, since they still have some degree of faith?"

Our human nature wants to classify people as either backsliders or ones who have lost their salvation. The issues in these people's lives are often issues of sin, not faith. We have somehow judged their sin to be worse or of greater consequence than our own. Reality states that all sin breaks God's standard of perfection. My white lies or someone else's immoral behaviors have different consequences on earth, but not in their ability to fall short of God's standard. If someone who struggles with sin is a backslider, then so am I. The true question becomes: how do any of us know we are truly saved? I do not doubt my salvation in the midst of my perpetual lies or pride, and neither should you. Of course, we should want to change, but the reality is you and I will continue to sin until the moment we die.

Our response to the one stuck in sin should be one of compassion. Let's not feel the need to classify people as still saved or not. Instead, let us walk alongside our brother or sister and help them through the struggle they are facing. God is the one who decides if one is still saved or not.

Having said that, let me clarify something. I truly believe continual, repeated sin with an attitude of unrepentance puts a person in a very dangerous spot. They are on the path toward a change of faith. Only God knows at what point this occurs. Again, I would say if people are unwilling to look at sin or make changes in their lives, they do not understand how great salvation is. They need to go back to school and relearn the basics.

I THOUGHT THIS WAS ABOUT BEING A SUPERHERO

Some of you may wonder why I am going into such depth to speak of the potential of losing your salvation. It is not really essential to our faith. We will meet people in heaven with vastly different opinions on the issue.

It relates to the hugeness of grace. If we see grace in its enormity, we will eventually approach the question of whether it can be abused or not. The answer is yes. People abuse the grace of God all the time when they commit horrific sin. But, if we are honest, you and I abuse the grace of God on a daily basis as well. Each time we sin, we spit on the gift of our salvation, treating it as less than worthy.

Let me relate to you a conversation I had with my friend Zac Eastwood on Facebook. Zac writes this about grace and the potential to abuse it:

"Often times I think people use the word 'grace' to mean 'mercy.' Like, 'I sinned, but there's grace for that.' As if God's standard is flexible, and He bends the rules for us. As if God says, 'Don't worry, I'll let that one slide.' But grace isn't God lowering His standard. Grace is God raising us up to meet His standard. Grace empowers us. We should say, 'I was tempted, but by God's grace I resisted and did not sin.' I think many people see grace as a passive force. Like a safety net that catches us when we fall. But I've been thinking that grace is actually an active force. It propels us into holiness. Your catchy definition is grace: getting what we don't deserve. Which is right on. But also, what about grace: God empowering us to do what we can't do on our own. The implications of this are tremendous!"

> Grace is an active force in our lives, not merely a one-time salvation experience.

Zac's comments remind me of Titus 2:11-12. "For the grace of God has appeared, bringing salvation for all people, training us to renounce ungodliness and worldly passions, and to live self-controlled, upright, and godly lives in the present age."

Grace is an active force in our lives, not merely a one-time salvation experience. It can be abused, but is the very thing that helps us to live and grow as believers. We will speak more of this in the chapters to come.

Takeaways

What are some of our takeaways in this discussion on losing salvation? As you can see, I do believe it is possible to forfeit or walk away from salvation, but it needs to meet the definition of apostasy. Even those who believe salvation is permanent can still agree with me on a few things.

First, I think scripture makes this an issue of faith, not sin. Sin is still forgiven and forgotten. Grace is big enough even in this age-old debate. Second, we should not change the way we treat those who struggle. Let's walk alongside each other and believe for restoration. Lastly and most importantly, this should breed security in our lives. We can have confidence that we are saved. I could fill pages with verses to support this confidence. Salvation is not a fragile thing that we need to fear accidentally misplacing.

As I grew up in youth groups, I heard sensational stories of Judgment Day. One particularly memorable version has believers who appear before the Judgment seat of God. Behind the Lord, is a giant TV screen that will show every action, thought, word, and attitude. Well, we know this is a bleak picture based on our animal cracker illustration. It sends tremors of fear through our bodies. An altar call is given at the youth rally and people are scared into the kingdom. Effective, but misguided.

If there is a giant TV screen in heaven as you stand before God, there will be one picture on that screen. A picture of Christ! Heaven and hell is decided based on faith in Christ, not our actions. There is no need to fear.

Not convinced? Listen to words from the book of Revelation. Who would have thought our youth group stories could be more sensational than the Apocalypse? Read for yourself:

> And I saw the dead, great and small, standing before the throne, and books were opened. Then another book was opened, which is the book of life. And the dead were judged by what was written in the books, according to what they had done. And the sea gave up the dead who were in it, Death and Hades gave up the dead who were in them, and they were judged, each one of them, according to what they had done. Then Death and Hades were thrown into the lake of fire. This is the second death, the lake of fire. And if anyone's name was not found written in the book of life, he was thrown into the lake of fire. (Revelation 20:12-15)

The dead are judged by what is written in the books. We know about the record our sins from our animal cracker exercise. Unbelievers are evaluated based on their actions, thoughts, words, and attitudes. When that is the case, the verdict is death.

Believers are judged based on what is written in the Lamb's book, the Book of Life. Their destiny is recorded in chapters 21-22 of Revelation, which is an indescribable picture of heaven.

Two groups. Two books. If you are in Christ, you have security and no need to fear! You don't need to be a superhero to make it to heaven. Jesus has done that for us!

QUESTIONS for discussion

Have you ever experienced the fear that is described in regards to your salvation? How has this discussion helped you?

Discuss the idea of grace training us to live godly lives from Titus 2. How does this affect your Christian life? What changes need to happen in your thinking to line up with God's Truth?

◉ ⊙ ◎

"I know of two alternatives to hypocrisy: perfection or honesty...I do not view perfection as a realistic alternative. Our only option, then, is honesty that leads to repentance...hypocrisy disguises our need to receive grace."

PHILIP YANCEY

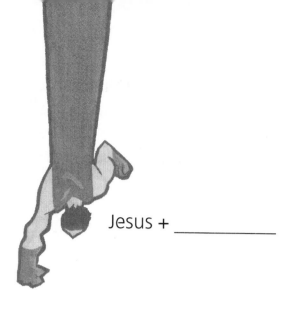

Jesus + _____

Remember where we began this book. I shared the story of one of my students who expressed "Superman is dead." The concept represents the battle that rages within each one of us. We feel we must be superheroes to live up to God's expectations. While we live with this focus, it is easy to get distracted and suddenly feel like God expects us to be perfect. Our focus quickly shifts from the gift of salvation to our worthiness of this gift. So far in this book, we have focused on what occurs at salvation. Now, we turn our attention to our part of the journey with God. We have the justification from the courtroom and the redemption from the slave market. Now we walk out and attempt to live out our salvation. The living out concept being dealt with here is called sanctification.

Sanctification can be illustrated by a tea bag. Imagine a tea bag being dropped into a cup of boiling water. We do not see many visible changes in the water the instant the tea bag enters it, but the fullness of tea is there. As time passes, the water in the cup begins to change; it starts to look like tea.

This picture is a simple illustration of the doctrine of sanctification. Sanctification happens as a part of salvation. The moment we exercise faith, we receive the gift. This is the same as being justified or redeemed. In the definition of sanctification is where we see its uniqueness. Sanctification is the process of becoming Christ-like. In the definition of the word we see it is a process. It would be correct to call sanctification a journey. The tea bag is in the water. All of Christ lives and dwells in us, yet it takes time for the water to reflect Christ. To follow the illustration, it takes time for the water to turn to tea.

Remember 2 Peter 1:3 tells us, we have everything we need for life and godliness (paraphrase). The tea bag is there, all of Christ is with us; we only need to journey with him to learn, grow, and change.

This is where the false belief of being a superhero comes in. No believer in their right mind would say the source of salvation was themselves or their own efforts. We can all quote Bible verses to this effect:

"yet we know that a person is not justified by works of the law but through faith in Jesus Christ..." (Galatians 2:16a).

Somehow after we are saved, we go back in our attempts to climb the ladder, using our best efforts to earn our salvation. Society screams these messages to us.

"Make something of yourself."

"Be the change you desire."

"Nothing is for free.""Be all you can be."

Everyone from Oprah to the army, constantly tells us the way to growth and change is through our own effort. It is easy to see how we get the message that we must be super-heroes. We know God demands perfection as his standard. This causes these tendencies to creep into our thought process. We must simultaneously be great Christians, perfect husbands and fathers, the hardest working volunteer leaders in our church, active in community service, and on top of that, good dog walkers! In short, the Christian life quickly reverts to being about us, and we feel pressured to be superheroes.

Paul counteracts this line of thought when he reminds the Corinthian believers of the truth. 1 Corinthians 1:30 says, "He is the source of your life in Christ Jesus, whom God made our wisdom and our righteousness and sanctification and redemption." In this verse, we see righteousness granted to believers in the courtroom of God. We see redemption being given in the slave market. In the middle of these two, we have sanctification. The first two gifts are received as a part of salvation. When does sanctification happen?

Most will answer quickly that it occurs after salvation. Yet why would Paul list this in the middle of two things which pertain to salvation? Remember the tea bag. Sanctification also occurs at salvation, but by definition, is a process. It takes time for us to look more like Christ, or, as the illustration goes, more like tea. There are many parts in this process. It is essential for us to see that the source of all life and growth as a believer is still Christ, not us. At the same time, we would never want to sit and stare at the sky, hoping to mature as a believer. There is a partnership in the journey. But we must never forget that sanctification begins with Christ at salvation.

Walking out of the Courtroom

We've been focused on the courtroom and the slave market, where God first gave us pieces of our salvation. Now, we begin to turn to our response. We know we already possess sanctification; we just need to walk it out. There are three main ways we can respond.

Response 1. Trash it. You receive the gift, but do not honor or respect it. A redeemed slave was not required to respond in a certain way. Freedom was so real, the individual could walk out of the slave market of sin and never see the master again. This is not the desired response to our redemption. I would argue that people who respond this way do not understand the magnitude of the gift they have been given. We must acknowledge that this response is a possibility, but in no way the desired one.

Sanctification is the process of becoming Christ-like.

Response 2. Pay for It. This response is quite common. We are grateful for what God has done, but now feel it is our job to pay him back, or earn the gift. A gift that is paid for is no longer a gift; it is a purchase. The Biblical authors never described salvation as a purchase. Our attempts to pay for this gift results in works, doing without certain things, or right lifestyle. None of these are bad. The question that remains is, "when have I paid enough?"

Response 3. The third response looks very similar to the second. You may even "do" some of the same things. The difference in the response comes from the motivation. When someone hands you a gift, the appropriate response in almost any culture is to say, thank you. You receive the amazing gift, treasuring it, as love and gratitude flow. This is the 3rd response—say thank you.

In the United States, we often express gratitude for something someone has given when we write a note. In this note, we express appreciation for what has happened. This is a thank-you note.

We can do the same thing with God. He has given us the incredible gift of salvation. We receive it and say thank you, writing a letter of appreciation with our lives. Our thank-you note to God will involve obedience, the removal of ourselves from sin, and doing the "right" things. It sounds similar to our attempts to pay for the gift. The difference now is in our motivation. We no longer do these things because we have to. We do not feel a need to climb the ladder to achieve some elusive spiritual platform. We simply respond with gratitude, as we desire to get to know the Giver of the gift. We do this because we want to. The gift of God does not come with strings attached. Remember, we could have trashed it, but why would we want to?

> Our thank-you note to God will involve obedience, the removal of ourselves from sin, and doing the "right" things.

Several popular authors have expressed similar sentiments in their writings. Philip Yancey tells us, "If I had to summarize the primary New Testament motivation for 'being good' in one word. I would choose gratitude."[15]

In his book *Ruthless Trust*[16], Brennan Manning tells us, "the foremost quality of a trusting disciple is gratefulness. Gratitude arises from the lived perception that all of life is grace, as undeserved and unearned gift from the Father's hand."

In the book of Galatians, Paul was dealing with a similar situation. He founded this regional church in several cities on his first missionary journey (Acts 13, 14). They were saved and experiencing growth. Paul continued on his journeys to others cities and areas. A group of false teachers followed in Paul's footsteps. They were called the Judaizers or the "circumcision party." You can imagine what their message was as you consider their name. They came and told the Galatians that now that they were saved, there was one more thing they needed to do. The false teaching they promoted was Jesus + circumcision. They went so far as to say, this was the secret to the successful Christian life. It is in the midst of this situation that Paul writes his letter to the Galatians.

Let's see if we can get a feel for Paul's emotions as he writes this letter. Try your best to read between the lines of Galatians 3:1-3:

"O foolish Galatians! Who has bewitched you? It was before your eyes that Jesus Christ was publicly portrayed as crucified. Let me ask you only this: Did you receive the

Spirit by works of the law or by hearing with faith? Are you so foolish? Having begun by the Spirit, are you now being perfected by the flesh?"

It's not too difficult to see Paul's feelings here. He is extremely angry. Nowhere else in Paul's writings do we see him calling a church "idiots"! Paul tells them they started with the Spirit, referring to their salvation, which had nothing to do with themselves. Now they had changed the rules and were in reliance on the flesh. We can define "spirit" in Galatians as dependence upon God. "Flesh" would be the opposite, defined as dependence upon works or self. Paul is going to carry this contrast throughout the book.

Why did they trust God to get saved but now trust something physical such as circumcision to please God? Can they be any more righteous than perfectly measured up?

Earlier in the book of Galatians, Paul equates the addition of works to Christ or a "Jesus +" mentality to another gospel. See what he says in Galatians 1:6.

"I am astonished that you are so quickly deserting him who called you in the grace of Christ and are turning to a different gospel."

Consider all of Paul's writings. He deals with gross sin in 1 Corinthians when a church member sleeps with his stepmother (1 Cor. 5:1). He constantly faces the mixture of Christianity and pagan practices in books such as Colossians and Ephesians. Paul faces dilemmas with people who have been poison in the church and have been removed (1Tim. 2:19-20). In all of Paul's writings, we do not detect the kind of intense emotion as we see here when people begin to add works to the gift of Christ.

Are we as serious about a "Jesus +" mentality as Paul was?

Let's move forward in Galatians as Paul confronts this different gospel of Jesus + circumcision that is being taught by the Judaizers. Galatians 5:1 says, "For freedom Christ has set us free; stand firm therefore, and do not submit again to a yoke of slavery." This has echoes of redemption and takes us back to the slave market illustration. The Galatians were set free from trying to measure up to the Law. Why would they go back to it? Works-based salvation is equated to slavery. By trying to improve the work of Christ with the act of circumcision, the

We can define 'spirit' in Galatians as dependence upon God. 'Flesh' would be the opposite...

Galatians are going back to the Law. It would be a return to the sacrifice of a lamb for every sin, or in our case, an animal cracker.

Paul really uncovers his true emotions later in chapter 5:7-12:

"You were running well. Who hindered you from obeying the truth? This persuasion is not from him who calls you. A little leaven leavens the whole lump. I have confidence in the Lord that you will take no other view than mine, and the one who is troubling you will bear the penalty, whoever he is. But if I, brothers, still preach circumcision, why am I still being persecuted? In that case the offense of the cross has been removed. I wish those who unsettle you would emasculate themselves!"

Wow! Paul might need some anger management!

The Galatians were living the Christian life well until this false teaching came around. The leaven Paul describes here is not a good leaven. It is the false teaching that has taken root and spread. These false teachers must have said that Paul himself preached circumcision. Strangely, these are the same adversaries who threw rocks at Paul's head in some of the towns in this region. Obviously they do not preach the same message.

Paul is fed up. At this point we see what could be a momentary lapse in Paul's own process of sanctification. We see Paul the apostle wishing bodily harm on these men through castration.

Paul, settle down now! Take a deep breath! It does not take a Biblical scholar to see that he truly hates this teaching.

In Paul's defense, I believe this is not merely an expression of his emotions, but a point he desires to make. Remember what act the false teachers were advocating as the way to a closer walk with God. It was circumcision. Circumcision is a small act in which one cuts a little bit off.

Paul has a suggestion for these fellows. If a little bit makes them holy, couldn't they climb up the ladder? What if they cut it all off through castration? If a little bit makes them holy, logic says the more one cuts off, the holier you are!

Paul's point here illustrates the dilemma we have when works are involved. How do you know when God is pleased? Is he pleased with circumcision? If He likes that, what if you go one better and castrate yourself? Maybe God would really be happy with you!

I have never been in a church service where the pastor promoted the merits of circumcision as a tool for spiritual growth. But, I have heard many teachings that use the same formula. No longer do we promote Jesus + circumcision = being a good Christian. However, the basic formula of Jesus + ___ = being a good Christian seems common to every generation and culture. Over the years, I have surveyed audiences regarding what gets placed in the blank of this equation. Here are some of the most common answers.

| prayer | worship | Bible reading |
| church attendance | tithing | speaking in tongues |

missions	spiritual gifts	avoiding sinful things
Sunday school	volunteering	obedience
Christian music	freedom	relationship not religion

The list could go on and on. Notice the things listed above are all good things. The enemy would never think to convince us that we need Jesus + fornication or drugs. We are too smart for that. But, if he can get us to do good things for the wrong reason, he will win.

Let's take one of the above examples: Bible reading. If your formula is Jesus + Bible reading = being a good Christian, how can you know when you have made it? Would it be a short 5-minute devotional in the morning or three chapters a day? When you are doing that, the question persists. Could you be doing more? How about 30 minutes a day devoted to reading the Word? Maybe you increase to 30, but couldn't you carve just a bit more time out of your busy schedule as you listen to the Bible on CD or iPod?

At some point, you will throw up your hands and say, "I can never be good enough."

Or you will just quit.

When a work is included in the equation for God being pleased, we must ask, "when do we reach the desired status?" When do we have the peace that is supposed to come with the gospel if all we see is pain, effort, and striving?

When is enough, enough?

Never.

Paul knows this, and herein lies his frustration. Remember what it felt like to attempt to live up to the Law in your own strength. It was impossible. Animal crackers did not work! God seemed cruel, and we wanted to quit.

Why do we walk out of the courtroom, and return to our attempts to live the Christian life in our own strength? We take the "climb the ladder" mentality into our walk with God. All of life and society says this is the way to advance.

Why would church be any different?

Grace breaks all the rules. Grace is not bound by human logic. Grace says the secret to the Christian life and being a good Christian is simple. It is not a Jesus + formula.

It is Jesus. Period.

I can relate to the emotions of inadequacy. I am of average talent in most areas, but not exceptional in any. I played sports at a small Christian school, but knew I would not even make the team at a larger one. Couple that with my less than average stature, and you have an adolescence spent trying to prove myself. I was always trying to be the nicest, friendliest, or most helpful person. It wasn't until years later, when I began to have a revelation of my identity in Christ, that I saw God's perspective. It was not based on my external performance, but in the work of Christ. Over many years, my thoughts have begun to change and will continue to for the rest of my life.

Mark Driscoll, pastor of Mars Hill Church in Seattle says it well: "Jesus plus anything is nothing. Jesus plus nothing is everything." Nothing we can do, pray, or give can ever improve the work of Christ on the cross. It is arrogant to think my little efforts could somehow enhance the work of Christ. Perhaps this is why Paul used harsh language as he called this belief a different gospel. Salvation is by faith, not works. Sanctification is an ongoing process of the gift received by faith at salvation.

◎ QUESTIONS
for discussion

Think about the significance of having sanctification come from God at salvation. What changes does this bring to your thought pattern, especially in the areas of "doing" your part?

Can you identify with the Jesus + equation? Have you ever felt like no matter how much you grew, it was never enough to be pleasing to God?

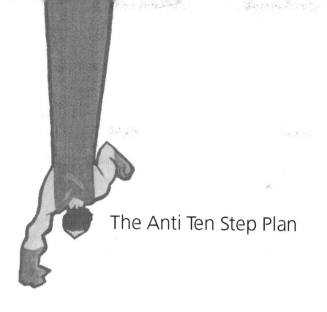

The Anti Ten Step Plan

Many of us have seen a series of books that include "for Dummies" in the title. We have *Macs for Dummies, World History for Dummies, Communication for Dummies*, even *Sex for Dummies*. It is easy to begin to take the how-to manual approach to our Christianity. We want the Bible to have a subtitle that says, "Christian Growth for Dummies."

We want a formula.

It is part of our human nature. Throughout this book you may have found yourself saying, "Great, but tell me what my part is!" To repeat the words of Bono, we have an inward desire for karma.

Ecclesiastes expresses this very sentiment when it says in 8:14, "There is a vanity that takes place on earth, that there are righteous people to whom it happens according to the deeds of the wicked, and there are wicked people to whom it happens according to the deeds of the righteous. I said that this also is vanity."

Grace doesn't play by the rules. Grace is not a formula.

Grace doesn't play in accordance with the rules of our society. It does not work like a mathematical formula. We cannot guarantee the outcome of life by living a certain way. Life does not work this way and neither does God. We may wish God would have a set answer like a mathematical equation, but he is not bound by any formulas. This is the basis for many of the difficult questions that people have about God. Remember the story of James and Peter? There was no formula for success in Acts 12; some live and some die.

I spent my youth in Lancaster County, Pennsylvania. There are gently rolling hills, acres of farmland, and the Amish, the main attraction for tourists. The area is conservative and religious. Even unbelievers subscribe to the motto of "do the right thing." This culture contributed to my deep sense of performance. This false belief system tells me I am only acceptable if I am a rule follower. This view worked for awhile, impacting my behavior and keeping me away from the really bad things. However the rules never dealt with my heart. Instead, I had outward adherence to the rules without the inward change. This belief system says if you keep the rules, you will be happy. I wasn't!

Sounds a bit like a formula, doesn't it?

At the heart of this belief system is a desire to control the situation. We want a guarantee of the outcome. If we boil life down to a formula, then we can control things. When we believe this, it seems logical that success as a Christian would be to simply follow God's rules. Grace stands in contrast to this and doesn't play by the rules. Grace is not a formula.

If there were ever an opportunity for a formula in Scripture, it would be in Galatians. Paul has just destroyed the false teaching of Jesus + circumcision. Now, he has the chance to tell them the true secret to the Christian life.

Secret to the Christian Life

"But I say, walk by the Spirit, and you will not gratify the desires of the flesh. For the desires of the flesh are against the Spirit, and the desires of the Spirit are against the flesh, for these are opposed to each other, to keep you from doing the things you want to do" (Galatians 5:16-17).

Wait a second! Where is the 10-step plan? Where is the formula?

Again Paul uses the contrast of spirit and flesh. The secret method he gives is to "walk or live by the Spirit." In other words, live a life of trust and dependence on God. Do not rely or trust in yourself or your own works. Do not go back to animal crackers! You got saved as you trusted God without any of your own works or effort involved.

How do you live and grow?

The same way: through the trust and reliance on the Creator of the universe. The rules do not change after salvation. Growth and change as a believer are products of a trust filled relationship with God.

Paul gives a list of what life looks like when we rely on ourselves or our works.

"Now the works of the flesh are evident: sexual immorality, impurity, sensuality, idolatry, sorcery, enmity, strife, jealousy, fits of anger, rivalries, dissensions, divisions, envy, drunkenness, orgies, and things like these" (Galatians 5:19-21).

Is this a complete list?

No. These are serious sins, designed to catch your attention. This is where people find themselves when they trust in their own strength.

Paul's demonstrates that the Galatians cannot lead the Christian life in their own strength or make God more pleased by things they do. Only Jesus can make us pleasing to God. Remember, he made us perfectly measured up to

God's standard of perfection with the gift of righteousness. Only a life lived in partnership with the true and living God can result in growth. Paul calls this fruit.

"But the fruit of the Spirit is love, joy, peace, patience, kindness, goodness, faithfulness, gentleness, self-control; against such things there is no law" (Galatians 5:22-23). When we trust and rely on God, fruit will be present in our lives.

FRUIT

I believe Paul chose the word fruit purposely. It is a picture of how growth comes. Let's consider fruit trees for a moment.

What does a fruit tree need to produce fruit?

Water, light, and good soil are all requirements. Branches that are pruned and a bit of fertilizer may enhance the production of fruit. These are all good, but are they the works by which a tree produces fruit?

Have you ever taken a hike through the wilderness and stumbled on a fruit tree? No branch is pruned and the soil has not been fertilized. Still, the tree bears fruit. A fruit tree produces fruit naturally. Imagine the opposite scene for a moment. You and your family take a peaceful walk through the wilderness when suddenly you hear a strange sound.

"Errr—I can do it—I think I can—produce fruit!" If you were to hear a tree utter this line, it would spark a hasty retreat!

175

Fruit trees do not strive to produce fruit. They do not worry about being good little fruit trees so God will love them. They produce fruit naturally.

That is what they do.

This is the illustration Paul chooses. A person who lives a life trusting God should expect to see fruit in their lives. It is the natural process of becoming more Christ-like.

◎ ◉ ◎

> A person who lives a life trusting God should expect to see fruit in their lives. It is the natural process of becoming more Christ-like.

Of course, there are things that can be done to assist the production of fruit. These are the things we call disciplines in the Christian life: prayer, Bible reading, fasting, etc. You can read the Bible all you want in your own strength. Without God who works in your heart, change will not come. God is the source of all growth and change, not you.

As a young believer, I spent many years using the fruit of the Spirit in Galatians as a checklist.

Am I loving enough?

Do I have peace?

How am I doing in the area of patience?

The repeated phrase and focus of my growth was "I". My walk with God was centered on making me a better person.

It is true Christianity benefits us as it causes us to grow and change, but it should not be the primary focus. Walking with God is not a self-improvement plan designed to make us better people. Christianity is a relationship with the true and living God!

Many of us have experienced frustration as we attempt to change ourselves in our own strength. We may succeed for a season, but there seem to be those areas where no matter how hard we try, we cannot overcome. We attempt to be superheroes, but deep down inside, we know we are not. The temptation to quit enters our minds.

It reminds me of an encounter I had with my son Garett. He went through a phase that all children do: the lying phase. When I caught him in a lie, I requested that he ask Jesus to help him stop lying. He did not want to. He wanted to do it by himself. Well, I knew that wouldn't work. He would fail in his attempt through his own strength. I told him it would be fine to try, but that if he could not stop, we would have to ask Jesus to help him. As you can imagine, it was only a matter of days before he was crying out for Jesus to help him.

Doesn't this sound like us as adults? Unlike my son, we strive to do it ourselves for a much longer period. There is something in us that wants to do things in our own strength. Perhaps it is the ingrained belief that nothing is free? Maybe it is our misguided trust in ourselves or the belief we can be superheroes? Just like Garett, we need to realize very quickly we cannot do this by ourselves.

The Secret to Wanting to Read your Bible
(and those other things we find really difficult)

How many of us desperately want to read our Bible, but no matter what we try, it doesn't seem to work? We lack the motivation to read it, so we don't. The tyranny of the urgent calls us to do other, more important things, leaving Bible reading to fall through the cracks of our hectic lives. Inside we know we should be reading it, but we don't. As a result, the Word of God becomes a source of guilt in our lives.

Can you relate to these feelings?

If you say yes, you are in the majority and not the minority. What is the secret for us to develop such a necessary, but difficult habit? It lies in our motives. Most of us have slightly distorted motives when it comes to these things.

Do we read the Bible to be a good Christian?

Is it because your pastor says to?

Is it out of guilt?

Maybe it isn't even as bad as these motives. Maybe it is out of an obligation to God. He saved us. Reading our Bibles would be the least we could do to pay Him back. Or is it as simple as the satisfaction that comes through the mark we make on our daily bible-reading chart?

All of those motives, while somewhat effective, are not the true secret to success. The secret to success in reading your Bible is not because you have to, but because you want to.

Seem too simple?

How many of you know when you have to do something, your immediate human response is not to do it. We hear the words "Don't touch that," and what do we immediately want to do?

⊙ ⊙ ⊙

The secret to success in reading your Bible is not because you have to, but because you want to.

Do you realize there is no formula in the Bible that equates being a good Christian with reading your Bible? Now before you pick up rocks to hurl at me, let me remind you that my life is dedicated to teaching the Bible.

So why am I saying you don't HAVE to read it?

Contrary to the way many believers live, the Christian life is not a list of dos and don'ts or rules and regulations. While there are countless references to things like this in scripture, they are not the primary purpose of the Christian life. These are principles to help us succeed and survive in the world. The primary purpose for the Christian life is a relationship with God. In unhealthy relationships it is possible to mandate things and force people to act a certain way.

In a marriage relationship, there are no requirements to love and communicate. You are still married even if you don't do these simple acts. Of course, to walk in love and communication with your spouse are good ideas. The reason you do them is not because you are married, but because you want to. Our relationship with God is the same way. We should do the things He asks, not out of obligation, but relationship. We toss around the word relationship loosely. How many of our Christian walks would be better described as an obligation, a contract, or a duty? If this sense of obligation describes us, we are missing the point. Remember our discussion of redemption from the earlier chapters?

Just as in a marriage you are not required to communicate, so in the Christian life you are not required to read your Bible.

Is it a good idea? Of course, I highly recommend it.

My point is if we are reading our Bibles for the wrong reasons, we may still grow, but our relationship will be drudgery and stagnant. What we need to focus on is our love and knowledge of God. One of the best ways to know God is to read His Word. Our motivations need to change. This change did not occur the day I had a revelation about my misguided motivations or the first time I determined to act out of desire. I had to wake up each morning and make a choice.

I used to read the passages in the reading plan and check them off. Somehow, that check mark made me feel good. But if I missed a day, I felt horrible.

It was almost as if I was trying to manipulate God, informing him my dues were paid so He should bless me. When I began to get a hold of this new concept, it revolutionized my life. I no longer felt obligated to read my Bible everyday. If I missed a day, I did not feel like God was lying in wait to strike me down with a lightning bolt from heaven.

The biggest difference I've seen is if I don't read, I miss it. I miss fewer days and read much more now that my motive has changed. The Bible has become something I long for.

Give it a try. I'm convinced your enjoyment and satisfaction will totally change. Instead of feeling guilty for not reading the Bible, you will find yourself looking forward to it.

Reading our Bible does not make us good Christians, Jesus does. Since he has already declared us righteous, the amazing gift will make us want to get to know the Giver.

for discussion

Think about how we tend to favor formulas or methods in our lives and how this creeps into our walk of faith.

Name an area of your life where you still do things because you feel you have to. Pray with another person for God to change your heart, asking God to give you a revelation of why he wants you to obey this command. What aspect of Him do you see in the commandment?

You Can't Get This at an ATM

I remember when I heard the story of people in Switzerland who made church benches. They took the finest wood in preparation for the bench and soaked it in a solution that would harden it for years of use. The wood soaked for 100 years! Imagine soaking wood for your entire life even though you know you would never personally sit on those benches! They were concerned for future generations and were determined to do things right, even if they never benefited personally.

Growth in our journey of grace is like this story. It takes a long time! This is consistent with the definition of sanctification being a process. The picture that comes to my mind is the same as the book title, *A Long Slow Obedience in the*

Same Direction by Eugene Peterson, author of *The Message*. I love this title! It fits so well with our journey of grace and growth in holiness.

In the previous chapter, I used the example of the switch from obligation to desire as I detailed my experiences with Bible reading. Through the years, I have observed some different responses to grace. They can be a bit like a pendulum. When we realize change needs to come, we swing wildly to one side or the other before finally settling in the center again.

When faced with the pendulum of grace, some swing to "I can do whatever I want." I think we have shown in these pages that this is not a response worthy of this gift. Others swing to "I won't do anything until my motives are perfect." Again, this is out of balance. Like my Bible reading, we still need to choose to do the right thing as we trust in God to change our hearts. I did not swear off Bible reading until I was emotionally ready. I read each day until one day I realized my heart had changed.

This is difficult in a society where we have become accustomed to immediate results. Microwaves cook our food. ATMs spit out our money. We can get coffee from a drive-through. Everyone is in the pursuit of a faster and easier life. Many nationalities have asked, "What do Americans do with all the time they save?" (Good question, isn't it!)

We carry this into our walk with Christ.

We expect change now! The longer it takes, the more discouraged we become. Many of us become frustrated that we have not overcome certain sins or struggles in our lives. We wonder if we lack faith. Perhaps God desires to do it for others but not for us. Doubts and questions plague us until we either give up or pretend they are not there.

Scripture presents God as miraculous and supernatural. People do get healed. Miracles do occur. But, we should ask ourselves if we have neglected another side of God that is equally part of His character?

He is a God of the process, who delights in the journey.

Little by Little

Have you ever wondered why God waited so long to bring Jesus into time and space?

From the moment Adam and Eve sinned in the Garden to when Jesus was born was at least 4,000 years. God could have fixed things immediately, but he was content to journey with His people until He decided the time for the Messiah had come.

All through the pages of Scripture, we see God is involved in the process. In Deuteronomy 7:22, we see God's promise to Moses about how He would give Israel victory: "The Lord your God will clear away these nations before you little by little. You may not make an end of them at once, lest the wild beasts grow too numerous for you." Surely God was capable enough to dispossess the enemies of Israel in a moment. Yet He chose to do it little by little.

In Proverbs 13:11, we see the same phrase, this time it pertains to our finances: "Wealth gained hastily will dwindle, but whoever gathers little by little will increase it." Statistics confirm this principle functions around the world. Studies of people who have won the lottery or gotten their wealth hastily shock us. Most spend the money quickly with nothing to show for it. God shows us He values planning and saving in our finances. Too many missionaries I know look with longing to the sky as they wait for money to drop. God can provide miraculously, but most often He wants us to walk in a journey of trust. Sounds a little like living by the Spirit.

God is a God who values the process.

The words of one of the most famous passages of Scripture confirm this principle is at work. Jeremiah 29:11 is a passage many of us are familiar with. We see it on our refrigerators and our greeting cards: "For I know the plans I have for you, declares the Lord, plans for wholeness and not for evil, to give you a future and a hope."

What a wonderful verse and promise!

We must look deeper to see the true meaning. This passage was spoken by Jeremiah to the nation of Israel.

They were about to be judged for their sins and sent into exile as a nation for 70 years. Look at the verse immediately preceding its famous counterpart. Jeremiah 29:10 says, "For thus says the Lord: When seventy years are completed for Babylon, I will visit you, and I will fulfill to you my promise and bring you back to this place."

The glorious promise of a hope and future is true! Yet the fine print tells us deliverance only occurs after going through 70 years of pain, difficulty, and captivity. Read the small book of Lamentations if you want to get an emotional feel for what this exile was like. Jerusalem was not a nice place to be as Babylon destroyed it and took the survivors captive. This passage is reminiscent of chapter 2 in this book, with a God who works for our good. That does not mean it will always be emotionally or experientially easy. It will be good, even if it means we must wait 70 years to get to the hope.

God is a God who values the process. He desires to journey in relationship with His people. He wants us to rely on Him as we walk in the Spirit.

BUILDING TO LAST

As I consider the last few generations, I often have a fear. I wonder if we will have what it takes to pioneer new works and ministries. That may sound harsh, but let me explain.

I have observed a blending of modern culture with our Christianity, especially in the Western world. This culture has decided that comfort is a high value and ease is a sign of success. In the West, people complain about microwaves being too slow or drive-throughs taking too long. Suffering is now defined as having a long wait in a restaurant.

◎ ◉ ◎

> We have allowed the culture of ease and comfort to determine the will of God for us.

I see believers who receive an idea or a dream from God. They immediately begin to find ways to make that dream a reality. Then a difficulty comes. Perhaps the results are slow to come. In the past, the ministry pioneers would endure and press in to see the dream accomplished. Today we assume it means God is no longer involved and so we move on to a new revelation from God.

We have allowed the culture of ease and comfort to determine the will of God for us. In this same way we have caved to the pressure from culture which tells us we must become spiritual superheroes. This same culture influences our view on endurance.

Will we pioneer any new things that can stand the test of time and difficulties?

The same is true in our Christian walks. God never promised it would be easy. Salvation often requires great sacrifice and cannot be interpreted through the grid of comfort. Success comes not when trials are removed, but when they are walked through.

Even our view of unity in a group or a marriage seeks to avoids hardship. This elusive quality does not come when everyone thinks just like us. That would be cultish! True unity is in diversity and is obtained through hard work. This is achieved when people of different opinions come to an understanding, working together for a common purpose. Unity is found not in the absence of conflicts but through the resolution of them.

The Africans I live and work with have taught me a unique perspective on this. If you listen to the way they speak of challenges, it is very different from those of us in the Western world. In the West, when hardship comes, we pray God would remove the trial. "Take it away!" In the West, trials are a bad thing. In Africa, these difficulties are a part of life. Africans expect hardship in life; that's all they have ever known. Their prayers reflect this attitude. Instead of asking God to remove the hardship, they pray for the strength to endure, to persevere faithfully through the difficulty. This sounds like a very Biblical prayer to me.

In scripture, we see God has the big picture in mind rather than just the comfort of the moment. In Deuteronomy

20:19-20, God tells the Israelites to go in and possess the land. These people have seen the miraculous deliverance of God many times in their lives. They may be thinking He will just wipe out their enemies. Look instead what He says:

> When you besiege a city for a long time, making war against it in order to take it, you shall not destroy its trees by wielding an axe against them. You may eat from them, but you shall not cut them down. Are the trees in the field human, that they should be besieged by you? Only the trees that you know are not trees for food you may destroy and cut down, that you may build siege works against the city that makes war with you, until it falls.

Is God really this concerned about the trees?

No, He is concerned with the future.

It would be much easier to wipe out all the trees as they capture the city. God, who knows the future, sees they will be hungry and these fruit trees will be of benefit to them. A difficulty in the present becomes a blessing in the future. God does not want them to mortgage their future for comfort and ease in the present battle.

Perhaps we need to change our worldview. Sometimes, difficulty in a vision being fulfilled may mean something different. Instead of quitting, perhaps we should be encouraged to endure. Instead of believing this tells us we are in the wrong place, it may actually tell us we are exactly where we should be.

What does the journey look like?

If you have made it this far in the book, you may feel like you want to scream at me.

So how do I do this?

Let me answer with a story.

I began my journey of discovering grace 17 years ago. As I mentioned, I come from a very rule-based culture. The freedom of grace was something that I needed. When I first tasted it, was like the sweet, fresh air of grace was constantly in my lungs. I would inhale deeply the joy of discovering the character of God and His plan to redeem mankind. My love for the topic grew, and I began to search the scripture from cover to cover to discover more of this amazing thing called grace.

I read everything I could get my hands on. Authors such as Philip Yancey and Jerry Bridges have profoundly shaped my understanding.

Then I took the plunge.

I began to teach on the topic of grace through books of the Bible and seminars saying things similar to what you read in this book. Each time, it was as if I spoke life to my own soul. I never grew tired of it. I am more convinced now than ever that this is my purpose in life.

Seventeen years and hundreds of teachings later, I found myself in an interesting and unexpected place.

The couch of a counselor.

All my life, I've struggled with issues of performance, feeling like my worth is tied to my output. I am a judgmental and critical person, especially of those I love the most.

You see, I understand grace in theological terms. I can give a very good presentation of it for people to understand. I can even identify in other people's lives when they are not walking in grace.

When I look in the mirror, I am quick to see my own failure. When I consider my own ability as a parent or my desire to be a good husband, there is always more I can do. As a leader and a missionary, there is always one more thing I could have done to help someone. Where does it end?

I found myself preaching about this amazing grace, but not allowing it to bring joy and peace to my own life. I was trying to be a superhero.

I was miserable.

This period of my life happened as I was writing this book, trying to be some sort of expert on the topic of grace. Yet, I had so far to go in my own understanding and application of grace.

So how do we apply grace?

Slowly.

Little by little.

By falling and getting back up again.

Sanctification is the process of becoming more Christ-like. I could not think of a better definition of grace. You cannot separate the two. Growth in grace is linked to our growth in Christ-likeness.

We may want a formula or a method, a ten-step plan to recovery. But God wants a relationship. God wants us to trust Him, to NEED Him. Each and every day, literally moment by moment. These are the words that Christian thinker Francis Schaeffer used to describe this journey. In his book True Spirituality, he describes the Christian walk as "*a moment by moment dependence upon God.*" Not month to month, or even day to day. Moment by moment.

How do we apply grace? Slowly.
Little by little.
By falling and getting back up again.

That's how we do it. As we walk in the Spirit, we trust him along the way. When a superhero complex raises its ugly head, we confess it, in reaffirmation of our dependence on God.

We will climb down the ladder, not up.

We must kill the superhero mentality.

Slowly, gradually, just like it is with fruit, we begin to change. God will be faithful to continually reveal new areas in our lives and hearts that need transformation through the power of grace.

Our job is to endure and persevere. We cannot give up!

Listen to the words from the epistle to the Hebrews written to a people who were ready to give up; to quit.

> Therefore, since we are surrounded by so great a cloud of witnesses, let us also lay aside every weight, and sin which clings so closely, and let us run with endurance the race that is set before us, looking to Jesus, the founder and perfecter of our faith, who for the joy that was set before him endured the cross, despising the shame, and is seated at the right hand of the throne of God. (Hebrews 12:1-2).

Let's keep our eyes on Jesus, the One who is grace Himself.

And most of all, never, ever forget...

We don't have to be Superheroes!

If you would like some guidance to continue this journey of grace, I would recommend you meditate on Scripture. Take Ephesians 1:3-14 as your first passage, but any one which deals with God's Character or His gift of salvation will work.

Read the passage through several times.

Make a list of everything the passage says about God or salvation.

Take each one of the words. Spend time meditating on the word. Ask yourself if you believe that this is true of you, or how God views you.

Look up other passages in Scripture that use the same term.

Preach the gospel to yourself, reminding yourself of the truth. Pray these truths over yourself until you start believing it.

Be Patient! Ask God to change your heart.

Repeat steps 1-6 of this non formula.

Notes

1 *Strongs Concordance* #4657.

2 *Bono on Bono* by Michka Assayas, Hodder & Stoughton Ltd (2005).

3 *What's So Amazing about Grace?* by Philip Yancey, Zondervan (1997).

4 *"Is God Really in Control?"* by Jerry Bridges, Navpress (2006).

5 *Sabbath* by Wayne Muller, Bantam (2000).

6 *Strong's Greek Definitions* 3083.

7 *Future Grace* by John Piper, Multnomah Press (2005).

8 *Transforming Grace* by Jerry Bridges, Navpress Publishing Group (1993).

9 Dr. Ron Smith Lectures in Lakeside, Montana.

10 *Strongs Greek Definitions* 2435.

11 Comes from various online resources and messages preached by Bridges.

12 *Breaking the Bondage of Legalism* by Neil Anderson, Harvest House (2003).

13 From the film adaption produced by Columbia Pictures in 1998.

14 *Strong Greek Definitions* #1096.

15 *What's So Amazing about Grace?*, Philip Yancey, Zondervan (2003).

16 *Ruthless Trust* by Brennan Manning, Harper, SanFrancisco (2000).

Interested in hearing more about *Death of the Modern SuperHero* and the topic of grace?

CONTACT PROJECT GRACE FOR SPEAKING ENGAGEMENTS AND SEMINAR BOOKING.

The teachings and seminars are available for:

Sunday Church services

Church & corporate retreats

1, 3 ,and 5 day seminars

Small groups and Bible Studies

For more information or additional copies of this book:

projectgrace@lautsbaugh.com

This book is also available
from Amazon.com and other retailers.

About the Author

CHRIS LAUTSBAUGH has been in ministry and missions for twenty years now. He has taught and ministered in over 35 countries. He is currently lives and serves in South Africa with Youth With a Mission. He is currently living and serving in South Africa with Youth With a Mission. He has spent years training international students in discipleship and Biblical training as they prepare to be missionaries. Together with his wife Lindsey, and two sons, Garett and Thabo, they formed Project Grace. This is a non profit ministry designed to help train and equip African nationals to reach the world. He has also published a series of 24 discipleship devotionals in La Biblia del Discipulado (*The Discipleship Bible*). Chris enjoys coffee, sports, and traveling to new places. You can follow him and this book on Facebook at www.facebook.com/nosuperheroes or his blog at www.nosuperheroes.com.

To order more copies of this book,
or follow Chris on his blog:

www.nosuperheroes.com

Project Grace, the ministry of
Chris and Lindsey Lautsbaugh.

www.lautsbaugh.com

Youth With A Mission, the largest missions organization
in the world with over 20,000 full time staff in over 600
locations worldwide.

www.ywam.org

To join Youth With A Mission (YWAM), the entry level
course is the Discipleship Training School.

www.ywamdtscentre.com

The School of Biblical Studies.
Using the inductive study method,
students cover all 66 books of the Bible in 9 months.

www.sbsinternational.org

Made in the USA
San Bernardino, CA
07 September 2015